PROGRESSIVE READING EDUCATION IN AMERICA

Through firsthand accounts of classroom practices, this new book ties 130 years of progressive education to social justice work. Based on their commitments to the principle of the equal moral worth of all people, progressive teachers have challenged the obstacles of schooling that prevent some people from participating as full partners in social life in and out of the classroom and have constructed classroom and social arrangements that enable all to participate as peers in the decisions that influence their lives. Progressive reading education has been and remains key to these ties, commitments, challenges, and constructions.

The three goals in this book are to show that there are viable and worthy alternatives to the current version of "doing school"; to provide evidence of how progressive teachers have accommodated expanding notions of social justice across time, taking up issues of economic distribution of resources during the first half of the 20th century, adding the cultural recognition of the civil rights of more groups during the second half, and now, grappling with political representation of groups and individuals as national boundaries become porous; and to build coalitions around social justice work among advocates of differing, but complementary, theories and practices of literacy work.

In progressive classrooms from Harlem to Los Angeles and Milwaukee to Fairhope, Alabama, students have used reading in order to make sense of and sense in changing times, working across economic, cultural, and political dimensions of social justice. Over 100 teacher stories invite readers to join the struggle to continue the pursuit of a just democracy in America.

Patrick Shannon is a Distinguished Professor of Education, Pennsylvania State University, USA. He is an elected member of the Reading Hall of Fame.

PROGRESSIVE READING EDUCATION IN AMERICA

Teaching Toward Social Justice

Patrick Shannon

NEW YORK AND LONDON

First published 2017
by Routledge
711 Third Avenue, New York, NY 10017

and by Routledge
2 Park Square, Milton Park, Abingdon, Oxon OX14 4RN

Routledge is an imprint of the Taylor & Francis Group, an informa business

British Library Cataloguing in Publication Data
A catalogue record for this book is available from the British Library

Library of Congress Cataloging in Publication Data
A catalog record has been requested

ISBN: 978-1-138-74233-8 (hbk)
ISBN: 978-1-138-74235-2 (pbk)
ISBN: 978-1-315-18239-1 (ebk)

Typeset in Bembo
by Taylor & Francis Books

For Ken and Yetta Goodman – Ageless Progressives

CONTENTS

PREFACE: THE STRUGGLE

> In many ways, *The Struggle to Continue* is my reaction to *Broken Promises*, a book in which I argue that the influence of science and business is the cause rather than the solution to the problems of U.S. reading instruction during the 20th century.

That's the opening sentence of *The Struggle to Continue* (1990), and more than twenty-five years later I'm still proud of the ideas and the analysis behind it. *Broken Promises* (1989) offered a critical argument that technological and commercialized reading instruction failed to deliver on its promises to be a catalyst for social mobility and civic engagement for all Americans. Rather it alienated teachers and students from the work that reading can do, denying the types of literacy needed to demystify schooling and the inequalities of American society. In *Reading Against Democracy* (2007), I updated that argument, adding that state and federal government funding and policies on reading education are complicit in the reproduction of a culturally, politically, and economically stratified society.

Closer Readings of the Common Core (2013) provided a single, 'textbook' example of how the nexus of these three influences has delivered reading education as a cash cow to entrepreneurs at many levels without addressing those unjust consequences. *Reading Poverty* (2014) took up the politics surrounding the fact that despite a century of reading research and billions of dollars invested in reading education, students from lower-income families (Carnoy & Rothstein, 2013) – confounded by race (Vigdor, 2011), immigrant status (Schwartz & Stiefel, 2011) and segregated location (Burdkick-Will et al., 2011) – continue to "struggle" with school reading. Although some schools have made modest improvements (Rowan, 2011), the overall income achievement gap has increased by 40 percent since the Reagan Administration (Reardon, 2011).

I've closed each book with calls for critical agency from "reactors and resisters," "critical educators," and "radical democrats," offering examples of teachers who refused to stand by silently while witnessing the effects of the hyperrationalization of reading lessons and profit motives on students and teachers. These agents used reading education to act in and on their schools, communities, and society in order to awaken and develop people's curiosity, creativity, compassion, skepticism, imagination, and agency. These examples were additional steps toward making good on the promises of reading in a democracy, but from book to book I did not connect the new examples to the century-long progressive traditions in reading education in the United States, leaving the possible impression that these current acts were disjointed and isolated events. *Progressive Reading Education in America* makes those connections explicitly and extends three important elements from my 1990 treatment.

First, I name and update the continuities and conflicts in the philosophies and practices among the women and men who worked singly and collectively to make reading a tool for the pursuit of personal and collective interests, desires, and needs. These agents are connected by their intentions to disrupt the binaries of mind and body, nature and nurture, and self and society, providing a not always linear path among the praxis of Jean-Jacque Rousseau, Mary Wollstonecraft, Frederick Douglass, John Dewey, Caroline Pratt, George Counts, Septima Clark, Ken and Yetta Goodman, Lisa Delpit, Henry Giroux, Vivian Vasques, Kevin Leander, and Gail Boldt and Ernest Morrell. We'll walk this path together.

Second, I use examples from reading lessons covering a 130-year span and much of the country from Quincy, MA, to Los Angeles, CA, and Milwaukee, WI, to Fairhope, AL. We'll listen to teachers' voices from rural and urban settings, while they work with children, youth and adults trying to help them make sense of their lives through reading and acting on what they learn. Although teachers and students have needed and will continue to need to develop appropriate curricula and pedagogy for their particular circumstances, they could and can build upon the experiences of progressive others. Those who seek alternatives to the current scientistic, market-based government mandated forms of reading education are not alone, odd, negative, or even necessarily innovative. Often unaware, they have and will continue to follow and expand a deep progressive tradition within the history of American education.

Third, I suggest coalitions among various practitioners of current iterations of progressive reading education, using social justice as a contingent framework. Regardless of their entry point or theorizing of their work, these teachers were/ are committed to the value of each individual, to his or her right to participate in the decisions that influence personal and social life, and to the collective struggles to overcome institutional impediments that exclude and devalue some people and/or restrain their rights. For example, John Amos Comenius's Great Didactic (1657) argued for (and provided methods to realize) a universal "climate of literacy" across social classes, genders, and languages, allowing the literate to "find them- selves all the fitter to use their understanding, the powers of action, and their judgment" (421). Writing as president of the National Council of Teachers of

English in 2014, Ernest Morrell explained: "it's difficult because we're teaching in an era where we are being evaluated upon constantly changing criteria … that's why I think we need to celebrate teachers who are producing self-actualizing seriously literate students who are poised to become authentic and powerful participants in our multicultural democracy … " (15).

The time between these acts might seem long, and the distance far; but their politics display similar commitments to reading education as a progressive social force for justice within societies built on privilege and profit. *Progressive Reading Education in America* surveys that time and distance in order to introduce such progressive teachers. Theirs is the struggle to join and continue.

If there is no struggle, there is no progress.

(Frederick Douglass, 1857)

1

INTRODUCTION

Then and Now

It is the advanced room of the lowest primary grade ... the teacher steps to the blackboard and with the laconic remark, "This is what I am thinking about," [she] begins to draw.... The room is perfectly quiet by this time, and she has the absorbed attention of the entire class.

"What is it?" is her first inquiry.

"Jumbo," is the instantaneous reply.

"Yes, that's his name, but what is it?"

"An elephant," is the quick chorus.

"Tell me something about him anyone." Then a storm of answers. "The elephant has a trunk"; "the elephant has four legs"; until fourteen answers are recorded on the board.

"Who can tell me what the elephant is good for?"

"To carry boys and girls," shouts an impulsive youth, not noticing in his haste that the last question was not to be answered en masse.

"To carry heavy things," is Maggie's idea. Just at this instance the gong strikes signaling the commencement of the school day. Group assignments are given and the teacher having seen the others all hard at work calls out the first group to the board for their reading lesson. Before the children have fairly reached the board, the teacher has nearly finished writing a sentence.... "What is it, Fred?" calls out the teacher to the last comer, unmindful of the flying hands in front of her. Fred who has not yet begun to think of the lesson, hastens his moderate movement and reads, "Who is going to Boston tomorrow?"

"I am!" "I am" shouts the crowd, thrown off their guard by this sudden question.

"Now, I am going to put on the board the name of something which went through Quincy very early this morning on the cars. Class, what is it?"

"Jumbo!"

"What's Jumbo, children?"

"An elephant!"

"Yes, and this is the way that big word – say it for me as I write – looks on the board. Who can tell me what I write now … Jeanie?"

"Jumbo is a very, large fine elephant."

Hardly pausing until the child has read, the teacher begins to write again, saying rapidly. "Here is something I want to know. Patrick can you read?"

"Are you going to see the elephant, Jumbo?"

These lines are from Lelia Patridge's field notes (1885/2010) as she observed Miss Bellamy's class in Quincy, MA, one Friday morning in May 1883. That's not a misprint; the lesson took place over a hundred and thirty years ago. There are some clues to the age of the lessons: elephants do not stir up as much excitement as they once did among school-age children and trains are no longer a primary means of transportation. I omitted several details that would have surely divulged the period of the lesson: 75 students were in the classroom with one teacher and two aides, the day began with a devotional reading of the Bible without controversy, and students wrote the lessons on slates.

Although the lesson was offered long ago, I was struck with how modern it seemed. For instance, the conversational lesson begins almost exactly the way Reba Pekula, the first-grade teacher in *Through Teachers' Eyes* (Perl & Wilson, 1986), begins her work on the fourth day of school.

"Can you tell me what I've drawn?"

The kids chimed in, "A bed!" "A pillow!" "Is that a dog?"

Reba responded, "Did you know I have two dogs at home and that they like to sleep on my bed?" Reba draws six dashes under the sketch and said, "I'm going to write something about the picture."

Cindy, a student repeating first grade, recognized the activity and blurted out, "You're going to put one word on each dash. That's how you write."

Reba smiled, "That's right Cindy. Now, what should I say here?"

Of course, these lessons are not identical. Pekula addressed writing and reading together, and she believed her students could write when they entered the first grade. The Quincy teacher considered reading alone; she simply sought to assess students' abilities to read "at sight." However, there are similarities, continuities I will argue throughout this book that connect these two lessons and others into the 21st century. For example, both lessons were predicated on students' oral language communications and their abilities to use that language wisely in meaningful contexts. Both teachers employed an informal approach in which they negotiated the content of the lesson, working from natural language toward consideration of its printed forms. They worked across symbol systems (drawing and print) assuming both to be meaningful and readable. They expected that their students would successfully acquire literacy and communicated that to their students through their actions.

Kevin and Krystal were second graders in Marva Solomon's (2009) digital writing workshop, creating websites in order to boost their interest and capabilities in reading and writing. Although the medium changes, the assumptions about students and their capacities to learn remain similar across the 130 years.

> In a traditional writing workshop, there is a share time, or author's chair that students anticipate and prepare for.... With online writing, choosing to share or not share is really out of the hands of the writer. The moment the students pushed "save" or "upload," their writing was available for anyone and everyone to see. Thus the online writing workshop generated strategies for controlling one's own text.... Kevin got into an argument with Krystal over visiting websites after he innocently asked if he could get a printed copy of all the student's pages.

KRYSTAL: "You mean of my page? Noooo. Can't you see? It's girls only. Boys not allowed."
KEVIN: "Yesterday, I went to your website."
KRYSTAL: "Oh … today, I'm going to yours. I'm going to get you. Kevin. (singing) I'm going to go to Kevin's website … Kevin, look what I'm on."
KEVIN: "That's not the one."
KRYSTAL: "Vampires! I don't get it, Kevin. You still believe in vampires? I think they are fake."
KEVIN: "You didn't see the movie I saw. Vampires are real. Used to be real."

The lessons have an authentic context in which curriculum emerges through conversation driven by the experiences and expectations of the students − even very young students. Their work together is meaning oriented − based squarely in students' lives, interests, and emotions (the circus, pets, and vampires) and their multimodal environments (talk, drawing, print, and film). Reading and learning to read engaged students in a continuous effort to interpret symbols in order to make sense of themselves and their relationships with each other and the world around them. These teachers assumed that each student is interesting and interested. These lessons and teachers share another connection − all were well outside the mainstream of literacy lessons for their times.

Traditional Reading Lessons

What makes the Quincy lesson even more remarkable than its modern connections is its stark contrast with the typical lessons of that time. In *Governing the Young*, Barbara Finkelstein (1989) uses nearly one thousand teacher diaries, student memoirs, and observer commentaries to describe the typical late 19th-century lessons. "Intellectual overseers" defined assignments, tested periodically, and commented upon students' abilities to absorb the content and perform the tasks assigned. "Drillmasters" organized exercises, choral chants, spelling bees, and other contests without becoming intimately involved in their students' learning. Overseer Alfred Holbrook (1872) remembered the guiding principles that he offered students just after they "toed the mark" but before they began to read aloud.

> You must not read too fast.
> You must not skip your words.
> You must pronounce every word distinctly.
> You must mind your stops. If you don't do better I will count for you at every stop: One for every comma, two for every semi-colon, three for every colon, and six for every period.
>
> *(p. 473)*

English visitor David Macrae (1875) described the drillmaster:

> In the next recitation room, where reading and spelling was [sic] going on, I observed the extreme care taken to give the scholars a clear and sharp articulation, an accomplishment in which the Americans greatly excel. Every syllable had to be uttered with as much distinctiveness as if it stood alone. "Rs" had to be trilled with more than even a Scottish clearness, making "tree" sound like "trrrree." The principal said the exaggeration was intentional to counteract the common tendency to slovenliness and running the syllables together.
>
> *(p. 475)*

Finkelstein summarized her sources:

> the evidence suggests that whether [teachers] taught in urban or rural schools in the North, South, East or West, whether they instructed students according to a literal, syllabic or word system, they typically defined reading as reading aloud – an activity which required teachers to do little more than assign selections to be read, and if he chose, to correct the pronunciation of his students.
>
> *(p. 49)*

Concerning writing, she reported, "In no instance could I find a description of a teacher who even hinted to his students that writing was an instrument for conveying thoughts and ideas" (p. 56). Overall, she concluded,

> There is considerable evidence to suggest that the typical teacher proceeded on the assumption that students were neither able nor willing to acquire the fundamentals of literacy without external compulsion ... which reflected the belief that the route to literacy was neither interesting nor stimulating.
>
> *(p. 102)*

Although the Quincy lesson was atypical, Finkelstein (1989) did find precedence for it, primarily in the homes of the wealthy. There, as in very few classrooms, Finkelstein noted descriptions of adults who "commonly reflected, expressed, and advanced a love of the culture of books and an affection for the social uses of the mind ... through a near constant incorporation of the printed word into the face to face culture of the household" (p. 125). "Interpreters of culture," as Finkelstein named them, acted as if the printed word could inspire children and adolescents to engage the world through reading and writing.

> The best part of my definite education I received at home. Beyond all civilizing influences was my mother's reading of Shakespeare.... I think I could not have been more than five or six years old when she first read *Hamlet*.... In the evening the whole family gathered in the spacious parlor and there my mother read an act or two of one of the great plays.... Shakespeare was an epoch of experience to me and not just a book.
>
> *(quoted in Hutchins, 1936, p. 38–39)*

Yet even the wealthy while at school "were to memorize and declaim, to imitate and reproduce texts, to repeat rather than formulate ideas, to recite rather than criticize a piece" (Finkelstein, 1989, p. 133). "If some were able to use the ability to read and write creatively, it was not because their schooling had taught them how" (p. 133).

In this context, the Quincy lesson stands out as an example of a different stance on leading students to acquire literacy. Rather than to relegate them to the traditions of the school in order to later fit them into a rigidly stratified society, Quincy teachers promised rich and poor students alike a voice in their lessons, and by extension, a voice in society. Their actions were statements about how children learn, to be sure, and they were also declarations that traditional schooling as an institution and traditional reading education as an enabling pedagogy had become barriers to recognizing the value of each student and their right to participate in a changing nation. In similar ways, Reba Pekula's emphasis on process and composition challenged the back-to-basics school agenda of the conservative Reagan administration, and Marva Solomon's new literacies approach contested the college and career readiness movement of the neoliberal Bill and Melinda Gates Foundation. In addition to a stance on learning, these progressive teachers shared a stance on what reading is for and what writing can do for individuals and groups in a democracy.

The Struggle for the Reading Curriculum

During the decades before the 20th century, it became increasingly clear that the traditions of reading lessons could no longer serve society because the United

States was changing from a nation composed of small towns run according to face-to-face contact among citizens to one based on growing urban centers organized around industrial and commercial interests. Changes in the social organization of the nation altered traditional family life and values, which further hindered children's chances of making sense of the world around them. An influx of millions of immigrants who settled in cities added language variety and unfamiliar customs to the cultural milieu of classrooms. Urbanization, industrialization, and immigration forced the public and educators to reexamine elementary and secondary school curricula in order to enable teachers to prepare productive citizens for the changes and challenges of the next century.

Although many agreed that changes were necessary, the purpose and direction of those changes were more contentious. What knowledge, skills, and values would serve American society best? Kliebard (1986) argued that these questions persisted across the 20th century.

> Rarely is there universal agreement as to which recourses of a culture are the most worthwhile…. Hence, at any given time, we do not find a monolithic supremacy exercised by one interest group; rather we find different interest groups competing for dominance over the curriculum, and, at different times, achieving some measure of control depending on local as well as general conditions. Each of these interest groups, then represents a force for a different selection of knowledge and values from the culture, hence a kind of lobby for a different curriculum.
>
> *(p. 8)*

Kliebard identified four competing interest groups struggling for control at the turn of the 20th century, and they are still competing in the 21st in the debate over excellence and equity in reading programs: the humanists (personified by William Torrey Harris then and championed by Diane Ravitch now), child-centered advocates (G. Stanley Hall then and Kevin Leander and Gail Boldt now), scientific managers (E. L. Thorndike then and Timothy Shanahan now), and social reconstructionists (Lester Frank Ward then and Ernest Morrell today).

Humanists

Humanist positions concerning change in schooling were both conservative and conserving. Advocates wished to maintain as much of the status quo as possible while still acknowledging the fact that change was necessary from drillmaster and overseer curriculum and pedagogy. The reports from the Committee of Ten (1893) and the Committee of Fifteen (1895) are touchstones of humanist positions on secondary and elementary school reading education. Committee members sought to preserve curricular traditions through the systematic development of reasoning power, sensitivity to beauty, and a high moral character among all students. Beyond the basic skills that enabled children to cipher, read and write standard English, students would study mathematics, geography, history, grammar, classical languages and literature, and the arts. "Every subject which is taught at all in a secondary school should be taught in the same way and to the same extent to every pupil so long as he pursues it, no matter what the probable destination of the pupil may be, or at what point his education is to cease" (William Torrey Harris in Committee of Ten report, p. 17).

In *Left Back*, Ravitch (2000) described the century-long progressive assault on the Committee's recommendations, leading, she argues, to the current crisis in education. Child-centered advocates inverted the traditional role of schooling from civilizing children and youth to fit societal norms to mediating students' individual creativity and interests. Scientific managers sacrificed initiation of all into the intellectual, aesthetic and moral traditions of the world for more effectiveness and efficiency of delivery and measurement of learning. Social reconstructionists insisted on equity at the expense of excellence, leading to low standards and moral relativism. Over time, Ravitch argues, public schools became more progressive, more standardized, and less intellectual, and as a direct result the knowledge gap widened between public and private school curricula, ensuring that students from financially able families would be much more likely to become truly educated than their low-income peers. To save public schools then, she maintains, we should return to contemporary versions of the recommendations from the Committees of Ten and Fifteen. For Ravitch (2010), The National Committee on Excellence in Education (1983) came closest to that move with the publication of the *A Nation at Risk* report.

A Child-Centered Approach

Child-centered proponents suggested that science, and not tradition, should direct school reform. Using observation and systematic analyses, child-centered teachers sought to support children and youth as they progressed through the natural stages of their cognitive, social, physical, and moral development. Traditional schooling thwarted this development, blocking students' basic needs for activity, social interaction, and authentic engagement with their environment. More than an attack on the traditional curriculum, child-centered advocates challenged traditional Christian views of human nature. Rather than act as if children were born in sin with a need to be civilized at school, child-centered teachers sought curricula and pedagogies that would help children to know and love themselves, unfolding their creativity, interests, and desires before they engaged with the competition, violence, and materialism of society en route to its high forms of culture. Control over written language through reading and writing, they observed, would develop organically as students discovered their authentic purposes for social communication, occupation, and civic engagement.

Leander and Boldt (2013) call for reading researchers and educators to reengage with an expanded view of child-centered approaches to reading education. Observation and analyses reveal that children and youth have different investments and interests around literacy in their lives. Its complexities are woven into the textures of their experience as they move about their worlds embracing passions and fostering both temporary and lasting relationships with other people and things. Reading and writing are an assemblage of practices that students draw from to negotiate their lives. Accordingly, humanists pay too much attention to the texts, scientific managers overemphasize the instrumental purposes of reading, and social reconstructionists concentrate too directly on harnessing rationality to notice what youth are doing with reading and writing, blinding researchers and teachers to the realities that students are not incomplete little adults needing to be assembled correctly.

Scientific Management

Like their child-centered counterparts, scientific managers advocated science as the solution for school reform. Rather than following the natural development of children, they sought to determine careful interventions and design precise measurement to determine the most efficient and effective ways to train students as able workers and productive citizens. Rather than through tradition, reading curricula would be developed through surveys of the ways in which adults used reading in their lives and the analysis of those tasks into their fundamental parts. Once a curriculum was scientifically determined, reading pedagogy would result from the identification, analyses, and streamlining of the practices used by the most productive teachers of reading. Test scores would determine which results would be codified in the technologies of teaching – textbooks, teachers' manuals, and assessment systems. In these ways, the needed changes could be managed responsibly, leading to equal opportunity for all American students to read and write.

In *The National Reading Panel Report: Practical Advice for Teachers*, Timothy Shanahan (2006) explains how lower than expected reading achievement test scores led the federal government to convene a committee of experts to determine the research base for appropriate reading curricula and pedagogy. Traditions and reliance on teacher experience proved ineffective and inefficient to meliorate the problems because they lacked objective controls in comparison with competing methods. Scientific research "helps to resolve this kind of problem better than teachers can do on their own" (p. 3), and the panel collected and disseminated the evidence for the scientific curriculum and instruction for school personnel. With that trustworthy and reliable information, schools could and would make research-based decisions on what and how to intervene in order to make all students proficient readers according to world-class standards. All other positions are based on personal, cultural, and political biases.

Social Reconstruction

Charging that traditional schooling, child-centered approaches, and scientific management contributed to social inequalities among groups, social reconstructionists sought to enlist teachers in remaking the institutions of American democracy. In order to help students understand and address inequalities, teachers would make adjustments in the context, materials, and methods of reading education. Teachers should take their children beyond the classroom and into the communities they serve, engaging the languages, stories, and cultures mixed within their neighborhoods.

> The materials of instruction must become dramatic, vivid, compelling because American life is enormously complicated and its ramifications are difficult to grasp. There are grave reasons for believing that it has reached an impasse and there is urgent necessity that large numbers of people, particularly our youth, be led to comprehend it fearlessly and sanely.
>
> *(Rugg & Shumaker, 1928, p. 156)*

With such knowledge and wherewithal to act rationally, citizens could achieve equity among citizens.

In "Skills and Other Dilemmas of a Progressive Black Educator," Lisa Delpit (1986) questioned the child-centered approach, arguing that its emphasis on natural development would leave poor and minority students without the cultural capital that corporate America required to be successful. With its emphasis on personal expression and creativity and neglect of inequalities, the child-centered approach would reproduce the economic, political, and social status quo. To empower these groups, Delpit called for poor and minority students to have access to the same curricula and pedagogies as the well-to-do, but with special attention to what Lester Frank Ward (1883) called the "artificial construction" of cultural, economic, and political hierarchies embedded in those humanist and scientific management requirements. In "Contexts, Codes and Cultures," Ernest Morrell (2014) explained that access, even mastery, of that content and those skills does not necessarily overcome conditions of oppression. To work toward participatory parity among all citizens then, teachers and students must ask and act on two questions – "how do I speak back to circumstances that I don't like or conditions that I feel are intolerable?" and "What kind of skills do I need, and how do I use those skills?" (p. 12).

Power Within this Struggle

Over the last 130 years, the negotiations over reading education have never been among equals. Groups have been more or less influential in the struggle over how reading will be taught, to whom, and in what ways according to general social, economic and political trends in American society. Humanists have dominated secondary school English education programs, partially and slowly accepting child-centered calls for individual expression and social reconstruction concerns about representation. To oversimplify, literature lessons added popular and post-colonial literatures and writing instruction permitted students to choose among topics and genres and to experiment with vernaculars and cultural modes. Yet the ability to parse serious, complex literature and to articulate text-based arguments orally, graphically, or digitally matter more than ever before from preschool through high school graduation (Coleman, 2011).

Scientific managers have been the most influential voice in the debate about elementary school reading education throughout the 20th and into the 21st century, bringing together three powerful non-educational discourses: science, business and the state (Shannon, 2007). Starting in the 1880s, the scientific study of reading played a large role in the emergence of psychology within the field of philosophy, leading within a few decades to the invention of the reading expert as someone who would discover and/or apply experimental results to reading instruction. E. L. Thorndike, Edmund Burke Huey, and William S. Gray were early leaders among these experts, who sought to achieve scientific certainty for reading goals, curriculum, instruction, and assessment. Moreover, the experts sought to translate these findings into technologies (teachers manuals, workbooks, and tests) in order to manage teachers' instruction scientifically. Professional associations of experts were formed to coordinate these efforts (see the four reports from the Committee on the Economy of Time in Education of the National Society for the Study of Education, 1915–1919). The sophistication and modes of those technologies have changed over time, but the originating principles embedded within them remain the same.

The work of experts expanded markets for these instructional materials, waving the prospects of profits before company, and then, corporate officials. From the rather humble beginnings of McGuffey Readers in decentralized school systems among the states to the multibillion-dollar-a-year projects of nationally coordinated markets summoned by the Common Core Standards, business has been a powerful player in the determination of reading education in the United States. Experts have developed ambiguous relationships with educational businesses, making innovations they hope to bring to the classroom through the wares of commercial publishers and manufacturers, while simultaneously lamenting that businesses base changes in their products as much on their bottom line as on scientific evidence (see Huey, 1908/1968; Gray, 1937; Chall, 1967; Anderson et al., 1985; Allington, 2002). Apart from the market, business practices have also played a powerful role in school reform generally across the 20th century, and particularly, from 1980 to the present. Since the turn of the 20th century, the success of tycoons and the emergence of American industrial innovations (Taylorism, then Fordism) captured the imagination of the media, which called for the application of the business principles of efficiency and effectiveness in all social institutions. From Carnegie

Units through the Ford Foundation's National Educational Television to the Bill and Melinda Gates Foundation funding for the Common Core Standards, science and management have occupied more and more space in school and classroom reading programs.

The federal government became a key player in reading education in the 1960s with the passage of the Elementary and Secondary Education Act (McGill-Franzen, 2000). Title 1 and Project Head Start were targeted specifically at reading programs. Although Title 1 did not specify a reading curriculum initially, it did require annual testing to ensure that the six billion dollars of ESEA funding was well spent. Project Head Start pitted different models of preschool reading education against one another in a full-scale experiment (see Rivilin & Timpane's *Should We Give Up or Try Harder*, 1967). American 2000, Educate America, and No Child Left Behind were successive reauthorizations of ESEA with increased interest in using science and business principles to improve state and local school reading achievement scores. Each echoed Shanahan's claim that science and technology would improve what teachers could do for themselves.

Because the federal government lacks direct authority over educational matters, it must use funding to induce states and experts to take desired steps. The ESEA offered federal funding for schools that would abide by its regulations. Over the last fifty years, federal agencies funded a variety of sometimes competing approaches to the scientific management of reading instruction. For example, the First Grade Studies, the national experiment to determine the best beginning reading instruction, ended with a modest nod to teaching code directly (Bond & Dykstra, 1967). The Center for the Study of Reading built upon that modest foundation with studies of reading comprehension, recommending equal emphasis on meaning and code in early instruction and then meaning alone after second grade (Anderson et al., 1985). The Office of Educational Research and Improvement funded research to follow the center's work (Carlisle & Hiebert, 2004), and the National Institute of Child Health and Human Development commissioned research based on the code emphasis from the First Grade Studies' outcomes (Grossen, 1997). Then, Congress directed the Head of NICHD and the Secretary of Education to convene a National Reading Panel in order to sort out the scientific evidence surrounding reading and reading instruction. The findings of that report were encoded into the Reading First Initiative of the NCLB version of the ESEA. The federal evaluation of that initiative found no difference in reading comprehension test scores at third grade between classes which employed the "research based" mandates and those that did not (Gamse et al., 2011). The Obama Administration changed course offering federal funding incentives to states that would adopt the Common Core Standards guidelines and commissioned two consortia to produce new national tests to measure the progress of students toward becoming career- and college-ready readers and writers. The first evaluation of that change in curriculum demonstrated a 30 percent drop in the number of students achieving "proficiency levels" with the new tests (Taylor, 2014).

Since the 1880s, child-centered educators who shared and share Miss Bellamy's, Reba Pekula's, and Marva Solomon's principles and those who adopted and adapted social reconstructionist values actively resisted the allure of high culture, the enchantment of one best method, the fascination with new time-saving technologies, and the attraction of the federal focus on accountability. That is, they struggled against the power of cultural hierarchies of tradition, experts, business, and government that have impeded the possible recognition of all individuals as worthy and, therefore, possessing the right to participate as peers with all others in social life. They used their relative power – their agency – to develop curricula and pedagogies that assume competence among their students, that center on interests, issues or relationships among individuals and groups, that seek authentic contexts for reading and writing, and that demonstrate reading can be stimulating for bodies as well as minds working in a variety of ways toward a more just democracy. In the remaining chapters, I tell the stories of some of these educators in order to help us learn about our teaching, the possibilities of reading education in the United States, and ourselves.

Let me first be clear about four terms I use throughout the book: history, progressive, justice, and democracy.

History

I chose to use the word story, rather than history, for a reason. Story connotes a subjective voice that directs the actions and thoughts of characters in order to construct a plot (Barthes, 1975). Typically, history is thought to be an objective description of factual events that are reported, perhaps analyzed, but not interpreted (Wood, 2010). Historiography does not appear to have a particular point of view or a goal beyond transmission of information. Stories enjoy such liberties. History seems to have a sense of rigor that stories do not. Yet, these distinctions might be more illusions than reality (White, 1978). Although historians strive toward accuracy, the writing of history, as with all writing, involves choices of topics, treatments and tropes – choices based, consciously or not, on the author's ways of understanding the world and her social theories of how it works (Hunt, 2014; Sewell, 2005, White, 2014).

Consider two histories of reading education that overlap in time periods. Nila Banton Smith's dissertation, published as *American Reading Instruction* (1934), has been revised and celebrated for eighty years. The International Literacy Association published a special edition in 2002 (with an added chapter to cover 1967 to the turn of the century from P. David Pearson). Smith's treatment of the topic stems from two basic choices. First, she understood reading instruction as a function of the spirit of the times – religion, nationalism, economic morality, cultural identity, and science – conveying an evolution toward rational progress. Second, Smith examined textbooks and technologies as the most revealing evidence of each period and of change. Barbara Finkelstein's dissertation, 'Governing the young:

Teacher behavior in American primary schools, 1820–1880' (1971), was published with a new introductory chapter in 1989. In her portrayal of reading instruction, she made choices, too. As her title implies, Finkelstein focused on the ways in which teachers' actions structured the possible actions of students and by extension the possibilities of their reading. To illuminate these ways, she examined the firsthand accounts and recollections of the daily practices in classrooms.

Smith concluded:

> As we review these epochs, we have a right to feel assured and gratified. Progress has been taking place all through the centuries…. Perhaps the supreme achievement for which this century always will be distinguished is that it brought to us the gift of scientific investigation.
>
> *(1987, pp. 424–425)*

Finkelstein ended:

> Teachers' tendency to rely almost completely on the texts meant that students as they learned to read, write, cipher, and draw maps, imbibed the moral maxims, the political pieties, and the economic and social preachments of the writers whose books the students were commonly asked to memorize.
>
> *(pp. 142–143)*

Although neither account is fiction, both tell stories. Smith tells the dominant narrative of scientific management in which technological rationality empowers all through an accepted vision of reading. Finkelstein disrupts that narrative with a child-centered perspective, allowing other narratives concerning the liberatory possibilities of reading to be heard. I intend to amplify those latter voices, narratives and possibilities because I believe that a detailed account of their intellectual roots; their theoretical debates; their daily lessons; and their alliances, divisions, and realliances can make a substantial contribution to the continued struggle to develop reading education as a progressive tool for social justice in a democracy.

Progressive

I label those voices progressive, although not all those teachers used that specific term to describe their work. I chose that label because the teachers share certain qualities that distinguish them from other contemporary teachers. However, I want to restrict the meaning of progressive to certain types of actions under the big tent of American progressivism.

> In the Progressive Era (1890s–1920), America entered a new phase of economic and social development; the old concern with developing industry, occupying the continent, and making money was at last matched by a new

concern with humanizing and controlling the large aggregates of power built in the preceding decades.

(Hofstader, 1965, p. 197)

Science and reason were to serve as levers to "achieve some not very clearly specified" outcomes of that concern. During the era, the nation enacted federal income tax, food and work safety regulations, women's right to vote and the national parks service; but it also enabled the creation of Jim Crow laws, the exclusion of immigrants, and the continuation of questionable science. "Urban reformers and pacifists and trustbusters and suffragists all called themselves 'progressives'. So did prohibitionists and segregationists and antivaccinationists and eugenicists" (Gage, 2016).

Although World War I dashed many of the hopes that modern humanity could learn to be wiser than previous generations, reformers and rights activists persisted across the 20th century and into the 21st. Currently two loosely coupled groups vie for the meaning of the term progressive. Consider excerpts from the mission statements from these two organizations: The Progressive Policy Institute (PPI) and *The Progressive* magazine.

> The Progressive Policy Institute is a catalyst for policy innovation and political reform based in Washington, D.C. Its mission is to create radically pragmatic ideas for moving America beyond ideological and partisan deadlock…. Many of its mold-breaking ideas have been translated into public policy and law and have influenced international efforts to modernize progressive politics. Today, PPI is developing fresh proposals for stimulating U.S. economic innovation and growth; equipping all Americans with the skills and assets that social mobility in the knowledge economy requires; modernizing an overly bureaucratic and centralized public sector; and defending liberal democracy in a dangerous world.
>
> *(Progressive Policy Institute, www.progressivepolicy.org/about/)*

> *The Progressive* is a monthly magazine…. We stand against militarism, the concentration of power in corporate hands, and the disenfranchisement of the citizenry. *The Progressive* champions peace, social and economic justice, civil rights, civil liberties, human rights, a preserved environment, and a reinvigorated democracy.
>
> *(The Progressive, www.progressive.org/content/about-us)*

By examining the language in these two mission statements, you can see that the tent of progressive has reduced its size. Gone are the racist objectives associated with the Progressive Era. Note, however, that the language of PPI seems to privilege the interests of global business over the needs of people. Moreover, the phrases "equipping all Americans with skills and assets that the knowledge economy requires" and "modernizing an overly bureaucratic and centralized public sector" are very close to neoliberal rationales for the educational standards movement that has plagued American schools for the last thirty years. As I hope I made clear in the Preface and this Introduction, I don't consider those objectives to be, in Hofstader's words, "a new concern with humanizing and controlling the large aggregates of power built in the preceding decades." In the remaining chapters, commitments to economic and social justice, civil and human rights, and a reinvigorated democracy are the progressive qualities that you hear in the teachers' voices and see in their "classrooms."

Justice

These progressive commitments align closely with Nancy Fraser's (2008) three-dimensional theory of justice.

> In my view, the most general meaning of justice is parity of participation. According to this radical-democratic interpretation of the principle of equal moral worth, justice requires social arrangements that permit all to participate as peers in social life. Overcoming injustice means dismantling institutiona-lized obstacles that prevent some people from participating on par with others, as full partners in social interactions.
>
> (p. 16)

I chose the three examples of reading education from Bellamy's, Pekula's, and Solomon's classrooms to show how progressive teachers developed pedagogies that disrupted, if not dismantled, institutionalized obstacles to students' engage-ments in the rich curriculum they offered. In each classroom, students learned to expect to participate as peers and how to do so – by raising their voices, making choices, and engaging each other seriously. The Solomon example makes explicit that all students, regardless of apparent ability, have the right to participate as peers with all others. That is, rather than pull the "remedial" students away from the web design until they have mastered so-called basic skills, Marva Solomon engaged her "struggling" students in the same curriculum as all, mediating their basic and advanced challenges as they arose while they produced their websites. To be sure, a major challenge to enacting a just pedagogy is to find ways to acknowledge and act on this fundamental principle of justice – all people are of equal moral worth and thus have the right to participatory parity with all others in the social life of the classroom and beyond.

The progressive commitment to justice influences curriculum within and among three dimensions. Fraser contends that economic, cultural, and political barriers impede groups' participatory parity. People are excluded, or at least limited, if economic structures deny them sufficient resources to meet basic human needs and to afford them time to engage in and reflect upon social life. Right from the beginning of the Progressive Era, progressives challenged eco-nomic barriers explicitly, calling for the redistribution of resources that would enable the poor and working classes to become full partners in the decisions that affect their lives.

Although Jane Addams (1899) called for recognition of the values of ethnic cultures, Elizabeth Cady Stanton (1892) proclaimed women were already men's equals, and Ida B. Wells (1895) decried the legal lynching of Black men, progressives' calls for the equal status for all in social life came about one-half century later. Here is a quote from the Progressive Party's platform for the 1948 presidential election:

> The progressive party holds that it is the first duty of a just government to secure for all the people, regardless of race, creed, color, sex, national background, political belief, or station in life, the inalienable rights proclaimed in the Declaration of Independence and guaranteed by the Bill of Rights.... The Progressive Party proposes to guarantee, free from segregation and discrimination, the inalienable right to a good education for every man, woman, and child in America.

The most recent dimension of justice, or rather injustice, concerns globalization and the geographic scales of the social arrangements that affect people's lives. Flows of capital, people, and consequences across national borders create new barriers to people's parity of participation because they obfuscate "the large aggregates of power built in the preceding decades." Progressives are challenged not only to identify the "glocal" connections between the local and the global but also to help people realize their political voice within the determinations of those new post-Westphalian social arrangements. This latest dimension of justice is clearly central to the differences expressed in missions between PPI and *The Progressive*. Progressive teachers ask who can secure justice across borders? And where does democracy end?

Democracy

This progressive conception of justice presupposes democracy – all those affected by social arrangements (institutions, norms, and practices) must share in producing and managing them. This is a remarkable and ongoing right and responsibility that cannot rest upon the authority of a deity, group or declared consensus. Rather it is a constant struggle among people to affirm and act simultaneously upon the equal moral worth of all, the promises of pluralism, and a faith in collective human intelligence to name and address injustice. That struggle requires more than any political form of popular suffrage in which the parameters of justice are left to elected officials. Democracy must become a way of life. In John Dewey's (1937) effort to make this point, his words convey the difficulties of the practices of justice:

> The key-note of democracy as a way of life may be expressed, it seems to me, as the necessity for the participation of every mature human being in formation of the values that regulate the living of men together: which is

necessary from the standpoint of both the general social welfare and the full development of human beings as individuals.

(p. 461)

Here the values of misrecognition embedded within the conventions of grammar exclude women from the category of people living together and imply some doubt about women's status as mature human beings. Progressives fought successfully against this exclusion as a macro-aggression – winning women's right to vote in 1919. Yet, these struggles still rage against such habituated and embodied macro- and micro-aggressions that make economic, cultural, and political injustices seem normal and natural states of American affairs today. Dewey cautioned,

> After democratic institutions were nominally established, beliefs and ways of looking at life and of acting that originated when men and women were externally controlled and subjected to arbitrary power persisted in the family, the church, business and the school, and experience shows that as long as they persist there, political democracy is not secure.
>
> *(p. 464)*

As you'll read in the remaining chapters, progressive teachers struggle to recognize and to enact potential roles for reading in people's processes of developing dispositions and capabilities necessary to engage justice and democracy as ways of living. (See my *Reading Wide Awake*, 2011, for my personal imperfect struggle.) Progressive teachers search for just and democratic curricula and pedagogies that afford learners the opportunities to convince themselves that they know enough to ask questions about any topic, that they possess the capabilities to learn more about those topics, and that they have the knowledge, the capability, and the right to participate on par with all others in the decisions that affect their lives. To convince themselves, learners must engage in the construction of the parameters of what reading is for and what it can do in their lives. And it works!

> Unused knowledge soon vanishes. Education lies in thinking and doing. From my experience in the progressive group, I believe I have learned to think critically and act more intelligently for myself. I believe that after studying in such a group, one could not accept a statement without thinking and questioning it. I believe that I have learned to read more intelligently and to enjoy reading more than if I had not been trained as progressives have been. I believe that I have learned to work with others as part of a group and for the good of the group, and not for my own benefit and honor.
>
> *(from an Altoona, PA, high school student's final self-assessment as quoted in Giles, McCutchen & Zechiel, 1942, p. 68)*

2

INTELLECTUAL ROOTS

I repeat that I'm simply trying to apply well-established principles of teaching, principles derived directly from the laws of the mind. The methods springing from them are found in the development of every child. They are used everywhere except in school. I have introduced no new principles, methods, or details. No experiments have been tried, and there is no peculiar 'Quincy Method.'

So begins Francis Wayland Parker's report concerning the 1878/9 school year in Quincy, Massachusetts. His remarks are both modest and defensive. Parker's appointment as superintendent of Quincy Schools in 1875 marked that school system's departure from the typical path of American schooling. "The set program was first dropped, then the spellers, the readers, the grammar, and the copybooks.... Teachers and pupils had to learn first of all to think and observe, then by and by they put these powers to work on required subjects" (Washburne, 1883, p. 13). Later, John Dewey (1930) would refer to Parker as "the father of progressive education." Clearly, there was something very new about the lessons teachers offered Quincy children, and Parker seemed to be the catalyst for these offerings.

Although the changes drew interest from teachers around the United States, who came in hundreds to see the "Quincy Method" in practice, Parker's curriculum and pedagogy also sparked concern from some Quincy parents. Many questioned his judgments and the claims of success for his methods. The renewal of Parker's contract was challenged in each of the first four years of his employment, and he narrowly escaped dismissal each year. In that context, his acknowledgement that he was simply applying other educators' scientific principles could be understood as an attempt to legitimize his work. Strategically, he grounded his work in an emerging European tradition, and he was quick to give credit to those whose principles he attempted to employ through the work of the Quincy teachers.

> It was two hundred years ago that Comenius said "let things that have to be done be learned by doing them." Following this, but broader and deeper in significance, came Pestalozzi's declaration, "Education is the generation of power." Last of all, summing up the wisdom of those who had preceded him, and emphasizing it in one grand principle, Froebel surmised the true end and aim of all our work – the harmonious growth of the whole being. This is the central point. Every act, thought, plan, method, and question should lead to this.
>
> *(Parker, 1883, p. 18)*

For Parker, harmonious growth required a democratic context – one that he fought for during the American Civil War. Toward that end, progressive teachers needed a philosophy in which individual freedom could/would lead to universal freedom. They found some of those ideas in Jean Jacques Rousseau's writings about education as first self-love, leading then to social understandings. Moreover, they needed philosophies that extended participation and enfranchisement beyond contemporary understanding of recognition and representation – advocates who explained that difference did not mean deficit.

> A school should be a model home, a complete community and an embryonic democracy. How? You ask. Again, I answer, by putting into every school room an educated, cultured, trained, devoted, child-loving teacher, a teacher imbued with a knowledge of the science of education and a zealous enthusiastic applicant of its principles.
>
> *(Parker, 1884, pp. 450–451)*

In this chapter, I summarize briefly the educational theories that Parker acknowledged and also those of three others who contributed directly to progressive education across the 20th and into the 21st century. These theorists provided the foundation on which Parker based his declaration that the "laws of the mind" can be found "in the development of every child." They sought to redistribute the benefits of education across social groups – many who were yet to be recognized as worthy of the benefits or capable of these acts. Each believed schools could be personal, social, political, and economic levers to develop each individual's head, hands, and heart, moving personal harmony toward a harmonious, just society.

John Amos Comenius

> It is now quite clear that order, which is the dominating principle in the art of teaching all things to all men, should be, and can be, borrowed from no other source but the operations of nature. As soon as this principle is thoroughly secured, the processes of art will proceed as easily and as spontaneously as those of nature.

In this remark from the *Great Didactic* (1657/1886, p. 252), John Amos Comenius offers several educational principles that progressives later adapted as their own. Most clearly, Comenius emphasized the universality of education in his intention to teach "all things to all men." Although Sir Thomas More (1516) wrote in *Utopia*, "all in their childhood be instructed in learning … in their own tongue" (pp. 182–183), Comenius set about the practical task of designing the school environment, methods of instruction, and textbooks necessary to undertake universal education. Pursuing religious rather than political goals first, he insisted on extending access to schooling. Despite his sexist language, he argued for girls to be enrolled in home schools because "they are endowed with equal sharpness of mind and capacity for knowledge" (p. 220). Additionally, Comenius insisted that the vernacular, rather than Latin, be the language of instruction. His greatest success came from the *Orbis Pictus* (1657/1887), a textbook to teach Latin through object study and vernacular translation, which he argued would give lower classes access to the knowledge that Latin encoded.

Second, Comenius maintained that education should proceed according to nature. Although a far cry from later theories of development, Comenius divided schooling into four six-year cycles in order to accommodate maturation. "A mother school (0 to 6 years) should exist in every home, a vernacular school (6 to 12) should exist in every hamlet and village, a gymnasium (12 to 18) in every city, and a university in every kingdom or province" (p. 408). The schools were to be distinguished from one another in three ways. First, the early schools would begin generally with an overview of all subjects and become progressively more detailed – "just as a tree puts forth more branches and shoots each successive year and grows stronger and more fruitful" (p. 408). Second, learning would proceed from sensation to more cerebral experiences, from concrete to more abstract concepts as students grew older. Finally, the schools would become more exclusive, with access to the gymnasium and universities being largely reserved for men of some wealth or remarkable academic standing.

Comenius's natural methods of teaching challenged the widely accepted idea that school masters had to be authoritarian and punitive in order to make students learn their lessons. He argued that the problem with traditional schools was that students appeared to need punishment not because they were depraved but because the curriculum and teaching did not always make sense to them. To rectify this situation, Comenius suggested a curriculum based on function rather than form. For example, "acquisition of other languages beyond the vernacular could only be justified on the grounds of utility and should not take up time which could be better spent on more realistic knowledge" (p. 358). Instruction was to be standardized, working through example if possible. "If you give them a precept, it makes little impression, if you point out that others are doing something, they imitate without being told to do so" (p. 216). For this reason, Comenius suggested multi-aged groupings so that "one pupil serves as an example and a stimulus for another" (p. 215).

Lessons in the mother school and the first years of the vernacular school were to be conducted orally, with explicit lessons on proper enunciation and grammar, in order to prepare students to know their own language sufficiently well to study another. Once literacy lessons began,

> exercises in reading and writing should always be combined. Even when scholars are learning their alphabet, they should be made to master the letters by writing them, for since all children have a natural desire to draw, this exercise will give them pleasure, and the imagination will be excited by the two fold action of the sense.
>
> *(p. 330)*

Beyond rudimentary lessons, "literacy should therefore be taught by means of the subject matter of science and art" (p. 331). Language and literacy were to be the tools with which students learned of academics and the world.

Literacy had a central importance in Comenius's vision of religious world citizenship. "We must not think that children are not able to take things seriously but in their own way. Children will be the successors of those who build church and state and they can become conscious of this through literacy" (as quoted in Laurie, 1884, p. 143). He considered a "climate of literacy" essential for full partici-pation in society, not only because it would afford universal access to knowl-edge, but "once literate, they will find themselves all the fitter to use their understanding, the powers of action, and their judgment" (p. 421).

Jean Jacques Rousseau

> I do not know what I did until I was five or six years old. I don't know how I learned to read; I only remember my first readings and their effect on me; it is from that time that I date without interruption my consciousness of myself. My mother had left some novels. My father and I began to read them after supper, at first only with the idea of using some amusing books for me to practice reading. But soon we took such a strong interest in them that we read without a break, taking turns throughout the whole night. We could never stop before reading the end of the volume. And sometimes my father, hearing the swallows at the crack of dawn, would say shamefacedly, 'Let's go to bed. I am more of a child than you.'
>
> *(Confessions, vol. 1, 1782, p. 4)*

There is some confusion about Rousseau's commitment to the place of literacy in education. Many think that he opposed literacy instruction altogether or relegated it to a minor role in the curriculum. There is some justification for this; Rousseau (1762) did make many disparaging remarks about book learning in *Emile*, his best-known treatise on education. "Reading is the curse of childhood ... when I thus get rid of children's lessons, I get rid of the chief cause of their sorrow" (p. 80). "Give your scholar no verbal lessons, he should be taught by experience alone"

(p. 56). "Things, things! I cannot repeat it too often" (p. 143). However, such remarks should be set in the larger context of his views on "negative" education, his own literacy, and his directions to readers of his novel, *La nouvelle Héloïse* (1761).

Negative Education

Rousseau understood society as an artificial product and not a natural association of human beings. For him, nature and society were opposites. He defined nature negatively; that is, nature was everything that society was not. Because he considered society to be corrupt, immoral, and unequal, then he believed that nature must be egalitarian, virtuous, and pure – a context in which human beings could develop self-love and self-knowledge. Because each individual embodied the traits of all humankind, Rousseau reasoned, self-love and knowledge enabled individuals to see the possibilities of human nature, leading to virtuous, egalitarian social contracts among groups.

Rousseau's educational theories, then, can be understood as an attempt to provide young children with sufficient time to develop self-love, enabling them to enter society armed with the desires and capacities to bring social change. Rousseau believed that each child was born to nature, with unbound potential for becoming a virtuous citizen. However, traditionally, children were immediately exposed to human foibles and social immoralities, eroding that potential and stifling development of self-love and knowledge. Without sufficient time away from society's temptations, children were unable to identify with the suffering of others, seeking rather to capitalize at their expense both early and later in life. Early traditional experiences perpetuated, rather than corrected, society's problems. Rousseau advocated for "negative education" in which young children would be kept from too much social exposure during the early stages of their development.

Seeing literature as an artificial way of coming to know the natural world, Rousseau's curriculum censored children's access to books because they would disclose the adult world to children too early. Rather than learn to read about the world, children should come to know nature through discovery and sensation. "Let him know nothing because you have told him, but because he has learnt it for himself" (1762, p. 131). "You have not got to teach him truths so much as to show him how to set about discovering them for himself" (p. 168). "Every state, every station in life, has a perfection of its own" (p. 122). "A child should remain in complete ignorance of those ideas which are beyond his grasp. My whole book is one continual argument in support of this fundamental principle of education" (p. 141). Accordingly, during infancy (0 to 5 years), childhood (5 to 12), and boyhood (12 to 15), the natural world should be the curriculum, preparing children to understand themselves and others as part of nature and learning to "read" the natural world before they attempt to read a book.

Man's proper study is that of his relation to his environment. So long as he only knows that environment through his physical nature, he should study himself in relation to things; this is the business of childhood; when he begins to be aware of his moral nature, he should study himself in relation to his fellow men; this is the business of his whole life.

(1762, p. 175)

Rousseau's literacy

The transition from childhood to adulthood, from nature to society, would be marked by a child's acquisition of literacy.

I am pretty sure Emile will learn to read and write before he is ten, just because I care very little whether he can do so before he is fifteen.... He learned to read late, when he was ripe for learning, without artificial exercise.

(1762, p. 81)

Perhaps the best way to track this transition is through Rousseau's literate practices as a youth. The quote at the beginning of this chapter demonstrates Rousseau's affection for reading. He associates his recollection of himself through reading with his father; he describes his immersion in the act of reading, and he explains their compulsion to share the experience of finishing the novel.

Later in his *Confessions*, Rousseau describes his introduction to the political side of society through an inherited library:

Luckily, there were some good books in it ... and I read to my father out of them while he worked. I conceived a taste for them that was rare.... The pleasure I took in reading Plutarch and the like over and over again cured me of any taste for romance.

(1782, p. 5)

Much more than an escape from reality or an opportunity for a closer relationship with his father, Rousseau found the act of reading (as well as the content of the texts) to be fundamental in his understanding of himself, his immediate social relations with others, and his imagination for possibilities within the society. "This interesting reading and the conversations between my father and myself to which it gave rise formed in me the free and republican spirit, the proud and indominable character unable to endure slavery or servitude" (p. 5). Reading became his springboard from thinking naturally and romantically to thinking socially and rationally.

La Nouvelle Héloïse

Rousseau conveyed his views of literacy and literacy learning through the characters in his novel *Julie ou la nouvelle Héloïse* (1761). Because the plot unfolds through a series of letters, it is difficult to distinguish life from literacy in this book. And literacy is a prime subject of the conversation between Saint-Preax and his Julie. Using the author's experience as the guide, Saint-Preax encourages Julie "to read little and to meditate a great deal upon our reading or to talk it over extensively between ourselves, that is the way to thoroughly digest it" (p. 56). Saint-Preax expands on the benefits, "you who put into your reading more than you take out of it, and whose active mind makes another and sometimes better book of the book you read." Not willing to let the characters represent completely his position on this reading, Rousseau instructed his audience in how to read his book. "This book is not made to circulate in society and is suitable for very few readers" (p. 5), he explained – only for those who could divest themselves of social sophistication and immerse themselves in the intimate thoughts between two young, virtuous lovers. Many found this type of reading engaging because seventy editions of the book were published before 1800.

Rousseau's contribution to educational philosophy is not limited to his thoughts on reading. In *Schools of Tomorrow*, John and Evelyn Dewey (1915) began with a thorough explanation of the relevance of negative education, citing Marrietta Johnson's Organic School in Fairhope, Alabama as a modern example. In their overview of the national survey, the Deweys discuss natural development, sense training, and incidental lessons from Rousseau's ideas from *Emile*. Yet, by page 60 of their book they seemed exasperated with the theoretical nature of Rousseau's plans and concluded, "If Rousseau himself ever tried to educate any real children (rather than that exemplary prig, Emile), he would have found it necessary to crystallize his ideas into some more or less fixed program."

Mary Wollstonecraft

> The conduct and manners of women, in fact, show clearly that their minds are not in a healthy state; as with flowers planted in soil that is too rich, strength and usefulness are sacrificed to beauty; and the flamboyant leaves, after giving pleasure to viewers, fade to the stalk disregarded, long before it was time for them to reach maturity. This barren blooming is caused partly by a false system of education, gathered from the books on the subject by men. These writers, regarding females as women rather than as human creatures, have been more concerned to make them alluring mistresses than affectionate wives and rationale mothers, and this homage to women's attractions has distorted their understandings to such an extent that almost all the civilized women of the present day are anxious only to inspire love, when they ought to have the nobler aim of getting respect for their abilities and virtues.

These sentences appear in the opening paragraph of *A Vindication of the Rights of Women* (1792). Mary Wollstonecraft had Rousseau in mind when she mentioned the misguided authors of books on education, and Emile's "perfect" wife Sofie was her model for women so miseducated. In *Emile*, Rousseau wrote, "Give, without scruples, a woman's education to women, see to it that they love the cares of their sex, that they possess modesty, that they know how to grow old in their marriage and keep busy in their house." Largely self-educated, Wollstonecraft sought support for her "revolutionary" position that women were capable people and were worthy of a public education. Seeking legitimacy for her proposal, she cited and extended the arguments in Bashuma Makin's *An Essay to Revive the Ancient Education of Gentle Women* (1673), Mary Astell's *A Serious Proposal to Ladies* (1694) and Daniel Defoe's *On the Education of Women* (1719), arguing for public co-education from childhood throughout adolescence. "I earnestly wish to point out of what true dignity and human happiness consists. I wish to persuade women to endeavor to acquire strength, both of body and mind" (p. 83).

Wollstonecraft wrote in the wake of the French Revolution (just before the Reign of Terror), advocating that the social experiment for liberty and equality include women. In the second edition, she included a letter directed toward Minister Talleyrand's *Report on Public Instruction* (1791) (still arguably the basis for public schooling in France), chiding him for not including females in the education for civil liberties. She wrote: "the neglected education of my fellow creatures is the grand source of the misery I deplore, and that women in particular are made weak and wretched by a number of co-operating causes, originating from one hasty conclusion" (p. 4). That conclusion, she reasoned, was based without empirical testing upon the religious metaphor that women were derived from, and, therefore, inferior to, men. She was not even willing to concede on matters of physical strengths. "Let us then, by being allowed to take the same exercise as boys, not only during infancy, but youth, arrive at the perfection of boys, that we may know how far the natural superiority of man extends." (p. 73).

Her central focus was that women possessed equal abilities to reason as men and should therefore enjoy the same rights as men. Wollstonecraft's writing perhaps provided the most compelling evidence to support her position. In *A Vindication of the Rights of Men* (1790), she outmaneuvered conservative Edmund Burke's *Reflection on the Revolution in France* (1790) rhetorically. She contrasted the republican possibilities of the emerging middle classes after the French Revolution against Burke's use of gendered language in his defense of aristocracy and privilege. Her first anonymous edition was praised by all reviewers for its ability to identify and expose the cruelties hidden in Burke's argument. However, after she added her name as author to the second printing, her book was criticized for the emotionalism of its female author. Across both volumes arguing for men's and women's rights, Wollstonecraft employed what she'd learned by reading philosophers John Locke, David Hume, and Adam Smith, blending their messages with historian Catherine Macaulay's gender egalitarianism argued in *Letters on Education* (1790).

Wollstonecraft tied her demonstration of rationality and the abilities of women as rational thinkers directly to the act and content of reading. Like Rousseau, she recognized the importance of the talk that surrounds reading, suggesting that the levels of thought required are modeled and set within readers' regular practices. In *Vindication of the Rights of Women*, she remarks on the modest benefits and profound constraints of learning to read novels.

> When I criticize novels, I'm attacking them as contrasted with works that exercise the understanding and regulate the imagination. I am not saying that the reading of novels is absolutely bad. I regard any kind of reading as better than leaving a blank still a blank because the mind must be a little enlarged and a little strengthened by the slight exertion of its thinking powers that novel reading may bring.... So when I advise my sex not to read such flimsy works as novels, it is to induce them to read something better.
>
> *(p. 102)*

Similar to Talleyrand, Wollstonecraft associated public education with the improved lives of individuals and society. In *A Vindication of the Rights of Women*, she argued that all human creatures would be transformed by this institution, fulfilling the promise of the revolution by creating twice as many new citizens:

> Asserting the rights which women in common with men ought to contend for, I have not attempted to extenuate their faults; but to prove them to be the natural consequence of their education and station in society. If so, it is reasonable to suppose, that they will change their character, and correct their vices and follies, when they are allowed to be free in a physical, moral, and civil sense.
>
> *(p. 131)*

Johan Pestalozzi

> The highest of all man's efforts must embrace all mankind, it must be applicable to all, without distinction of zones, or nations in which they may be born. It must acknowledge the rights of man in the fullest sense of the word.
>
> *(Pestalozzi, 1827, p. 88)*

> I believe it is not possible for common popular instruction to advance a step, so long as formulas of instruction are not found which make the teacher, at least in the elementary stages of knowledge, merely the mechanical tool of a method, the result of which springs from the nature of the formulas and not from the skill of the man who uses it.
>
> *(Pestalozzi, 1801, p. 41)*

Johan Pestalozzi translated Comenius's and Rousseau's theories into the daily practice of providing lessons that would enable indigent youth to become self-sufficient economically, morally, and socially. Pestalozzi considered Rousseau's "negative education" to be impractical for all but the rich and Comenius's too dependent on the quality of the teacher. To compensate, Pestalozzi based his schools on love and support for children in order to extend the necessary security to develop self-love within the hardships and temptations of children's everyday lives. Extending the notion that Emile should engage in manual as well as mental work, Pestalozzi used objects from children's immediate environments to develop students' technical and intellectual faculties.

He began in Neuhof, Switzerland (1774–1779), using farming, a spinning mill, and handicrafts as the tools for formal lessons. In his first book, *Leonard and Gertrude* (1780), he expanded his principles of personal development of the poor to a social doctrine – a fictionalized account of how a school such as his could revitalize a town through well-designed lessons. In a sequel, *How Gertrude Teaches Her Children* (1801), Pestalozzi focused directly on the psychology of teaching required to help poor students learn. In the latter work, his place-based curriculum gave way to more detailed accounts of how teachers could organize their lessons in order to transfer information and skills from the teacher to his students. Teachers were to analyze every object, every task, every idea for their schematic structure of elemental parts, and then, set these parts in a logical sequence of lessons to be taught. Pestalozzi emphasized that teachers should always work from the simplest to the most complex and from the most general to the most specific in order to be successful. Reading began with Comenius's labels for things, followed by teachers analyzing the words to its component letters to teach their shapes and sounds. Once mastered the letters were reassembled to create syllables, words for labeling other objects.

William Maclure led the first efforts to introduce Pestalozzism in the United States, bringing Joseph Neef, one of Pestalozzi's co-teachers, to Philadelphia in 1805, publishing his *Sketch of a Plan and Method of Education* in 1808; and organizing and financing the school for the utopian social experiment in New Harmony, Indiana (1825–1828). Maclure (1831) was attracted to Pestalozzi's conviction to redistribute knowledge more broadly in society. He wrote, "knowledge is power in political societies" (p. 5), yet it was denied to the productive (working) classes and controlled by the unproductive (ruling) classes. Maclure argued that this made the majority dependent on a wealthy minority, a distinction that served a democracy poorly. The answer, he reasoned, was education.

> For this 30 years, I have considered ignorance as the cause of all the miseries and errors of mankind and have used all my endeavors to reduce the quantity of that truly disabled evil. My experience soon convinced me that it was impossible to give any real information to men, and that the only possible means of giving useful knowledge to the world was by the education of children. About 15 years ago, I stumbled on the Pestalozzian system, which appeared to me to be the best that I had seen for the diffusion of useful knowledge.
>
> *(Maclure, 1820, p. 301)*

Maclure defined useful knowledge in two ways. First, useful knowledge has immediate social utility, and Pestalozzi's combination of labor and academics afforded both the setting and the opportunity for all classes to reexamine and study the familiar. Second, useful knowledge would help individuals become economically and politically productive citizens. Useless knowledge – abstract and arcane skills and information – was an artificial barrier that the unproductive classes used to keep the productive classes from sharing power. Pestalozzi offered the vehicle to change schools, and then society – at least in New Harmony.

Edward A. Sheldon took a different approach to bring Pestalozzism to the United States. While inspecting Toronto schools in 1860, he purchased $300 worth of instructional materials (objects, images, and teacher's manuals) from the Canadian English Home and Colonial Infant and Juvenile School Society in order to retrain the teachers of Oswego, New York. He rewrote the school district's course of study for teachers in order to include elements he attributed to Pestalozzi. The following year, he established the Oswego State Normal and Training School (Now SUNY Oswego), hiring a teacher from the Home and Colonial Society in order to provide pre-service and in-service teachers with Pestalozzi training. Dearborn (1925), and later Cuban (1984) attributed most of Pestalozzi's influence in America to the "Oswego Movement" because it could be easily adapted by the overseers and drillmasters who populated classrooms during the second half of the 19th century.

Friedrich Froebel

> We grant space and time to young plants and animals because we know that, in accordance with the laws that live in them, they will develop properly and grow well; young animals and plants are given rest, and arbitrary interference with their growth is avoided, because it is known that the opposite practice would disturb their pure unfolding and sound development; but the young human being is looked upon as a piece of wax, a lump of clay which man can mold into what he pleases.

In this statement from *The Education of Man* (1826), Froebel used the Rousseauian metaphor of nature to provide the rationale for "kinder" "garten" in order to address Pestalozzi's tension between knowledge as power and the power of pedagogical method. After reading *How Gertrude Teaches her Children*, Froebel served as an intern for Pestalozzi at Yverdon from 1808 to 1810, leaving that service with the conviction that Pestalozzi had lost sight of the theoretical in order to hone his methods. To prevent this criticism of his own efforts in education, Froebel made his philosophical framework – a search for unity between humankind and nature through the harmonious development of the whole child, body, soul, and intellect – the cornerstone of each document and school practice.

Froebel's conception of education is based loosely on Hegel's attempt to reconcile Kant's duality of pure reason (material nature) and practical reason (thought and morality) through a dialectical movement toward a comprehensive unity. According to Froebel, this unity could only be achieved through the study and struggle between the personal and the social world within each person. "Everything and every being comes to be known only as it is connected with the opposite of its kind, and as its unity, its agreement with its opposite is discovered." (p. 42). He argued that language is the primary mediator in this dialectic. "A man's speech should be, as it were, his self in its integrity.... It will reveal also the character of nature as a whole. It will become an image of man's inner and outer world" (p. 211). Language, then, becomes the means through which "to reveal the inner, to make the internal external, the external internal, and to show both the internal and external in the natural, primordial, necessary harmony and unity" (p. 209).

The use of language presents another dialectic struggle, one between the speaker's "self active outward expression of the inner" and her attempts to capture the essence of the natural and social outer world. "All laws of the inner and outer worlds, collectively and singly, must be revealed in language, must lie in language itself" (p. 211). These laws need not be consciously recognized, but through the dialectic of language in use, they are practiced regularly. Froebel employed an analogy to make this point: "Although the amateur musician knows and can say but little concerning the musical laws ... he sees necessity and conforms to law at every step of a great musical production in spite of all its apparent freedom" (p. 214). His steps from language to literacy, according to Froebel are logical and self-induced.

> Man in the midst of life finds himself unable to hold fast for himself and his memory, the great number of facts ... and one experience seems to displace another. And this is well for this awakens in him the irresistible impulse and imperative need to snatch from oblivion for himself and others the blossoms and fruits of the rich but passing inner life, and to hold fast by means of external symbols the fleeting external life in shape, place, time, and other circumstances.
>
> *(p. 221)*

Froebel found the catalyst for literacy in the unity of opposites between the individual's need to make sense of her experience (to construct memory) and the complexities and constant demands of the outer world. The need for literacy, then, stems from the richness of inner experiences. At school, a literacy curriculum would start with spiritual (inner) development to be followed by sensational (outer) exploration of nature. Contrary to Rousseau's isolation for Emile, Froebel's students experienced these acts in social contexts inviting them to express their understandings orally. In time, these acts would create a spontaneous "need" for written language. Although Froebel cautioned parents and teachers not to neglect the inner life or to rush to formal lessons, he followed Pestalozzi's sequence for written language curriculum once an inner interest was expressed – from phonology to graphology to spelling of words to phrases, sentences, and beyond over time.

> Here we see a boy making a sketch of the apple tree on which he discovered a nest with young birds, there another busy over the picture of a kite he sent up high into the air.... Another asks for some paper to write a letter to father. The little boy is urged to this by the intensity of his inner life, which he would communicate. It is not imitation, he has seen no one writing, but he knows he can gratify his desire. To him his marks, resembling one another quite closely, mean different words, which he intended to write to the person addressed, and we see here a manifestation of the inner desire for symbolic writing, as in the former cases his inner desire for pictorial writing was shown.
>
> *(p. 222–223)*

In order to promote an institutional version of negative education in which young children would not be pressured toward social conformity, Froebel proposed, implemented and developed "the kindergarten." In 1839, he opened his first institution for early childhood education, calling it the Play and Activity Institute. By 1840, he changed the name to the Universal German Kindergarten, staffing it entirely with female teachers who had been trained to provide young children (kinder) an environment in which they could explore and talk about the natural world (garten). The curriculum required children to act, observe, understand and apply knowledge and to analyze, synthesize, and evaluate their experiences. Because the outcomes could not be predetermined, Froebel considered kindergarten to be the beginning of the development of inner lives that could challenge and change the rigidities of social life. Accordingly, he referred to kindergarten as "the free republic of childhood."

Frederick Douglass

> Give the Negro fair play and let him alone. I meant all that I said and a good deal more than some understand by fair play. It is not fair play to start the Negro out in life, for nothing and with nothing, while others start with the advantage of a thousand years behind them … . Should the American people put a school house in every valley of the South and a church on every hill side and supply the one with teachers and other with preachers, for a hundred years to come, they would not then have given fair play to the Negro. The nearest approach to justice to the Negro for the past is to do him justice in the present. Throw open to him the doors of the schools, the factories, the workshops, and of all mechanical industries. For his own welfare, give him a chance to do whatever he can do well. If he fails then, let him fail! I can, however, assure you that he will not fail.
>
> *(Douglass, 1894a)*

Frederick Douglass offered these words of correction during a speech at the Indian Industrial School at Carlisle, Pennsylvania, in 1894. He was responding to misrepresentations of his turn of phrase, "give fair play and let him alone," from his many versions of his speech, "Self Made Men." Others had interpreted his statement to mean that emancipation offered African Americans the equal opportunities to take advantage of what society had to offer. Therefore, no further action was needed or warranted. Douglass explained that these interpretations ignored both the social advantages that white citizens enjoyed as a birthright, and the systematic denial through custom and law of those advantages to African Americans. In reality, he implied, the starting points of the two groups were unequal, and therefore, could not reasonably considered to be fair. If society were to become fair, then African Americans would enjoy the same social advantages as their white peers, and under those conditions, Douglass assumed both groups would be equally successful.

In order to achieve fairness, Douglass argued, the color line had to be erased from the United States. White citizens must accept all human beings, recognizing their equal moral worth, and therefore, their rights to participate in society as peers. Douglass believed the abolitionists were examples for the beginning of this required movement:

> They saw in the slave, manhood, brotherhood, and womanhood outraged, neglected and degraded, and their own noble manhood, not their racehood, revolted at the offense. They placed the emphasis where it belonged, not on the mint, anise and cumin of race and color, but upon manhood, and the weightier matters of the law ... . Whoever is for equal rights, for equal education, for equal opportunities for all men, of whatever race or color – I hail him as a 'countryman, clansman, kinsman, and brother beloved.'
>
> *(1894b)*

In order to participate in society as an equal, according to Douglass, African Americans must take full advantage of all opportunities available. For Douglass, education was foremost among life's opportunities: "To deny education to any people is one of the greatest crimes against human nature."

Formal education would enable the latent possibilities that had been denied systematically to slaves, and then, neglected after emancipation. Developing their intellects at school would prepare African Americans to compete for "all profitable employments;" to develop their capacities for "good citizenship;" and to "uplift them into the glorious light of truth." And for Douglass, these possibilities began when he learned to read and write, encountering ideas beyond his immediate censored context and leading him to express how those ideas might be put to use in order to enhance life's possibilities for others and himself. His literacy had been useful on multiple levels – instrumentally (he forged documents to gain his freedom), economically (his *Narrative of the Life of Frederick Douglass* was a bestseller and gained him employment as an abolitionist speaker), and politically (he wrote and edited *The North Star* – "Right is of no sex/Truth is of no color/God is the father of us all, and we are all brethren").

This very success, Douglass reasoned, would "invite repression" from white citizens, who feared fair play and its likely outcomes.

> The negro in ignorance and rags meets no resistance.... It is only when he acquires education, property, popularity and influence. Only when he attempts to rise above his ancient level, where he was numbered with the beast in the field, and aspires to be a man and a man among men, that he invites repression.... He meets with resistance now, because he is now, more than ever, fitting himself for a higher life.
>
> *(Douglass, 1894b)*

In the face of this resistance, Douglass understood the segregated industrial schools for African Americans across many states (even in the South) and the boarding schools for Native Americans to be modest steps toward the recognition of all people. As the quote at the beginning of the section attests, however, he believed that fair play would not be possible until all classrooms were open to all groups and teachers considered the relative advantages and disadvantages of each student when planning appropriate curriculum and pedagogy for their harmonious development.

Well-established Principles of Teaching

Francis Parker grounded his suggestions to Quincy teachers within the assumptions that were to become the foundation of the child-centered and social reconstructionist approaches to progressive education. Schools were to provide environments for learners and their teachers to create egalitarian dispositions who would become agents for change. Children were to be the center of their education as they progressed naturally through the stages of development. Although there was not consensus on the length or parameters of these stages, each reformer acknowledged that children and adolescents possessed special logics that should not be under- or overestimated or conflated with adults' thinking. Through careful observations, teachers would recognize each child's intellectual, moral, and physical development, using the child's interests and play to provide a unified curriculum for his or her advancement. Although not completely devoid of drill and routine, teachers were to encourage students' self-activity and control, refraining from coercion and punishment. Parker, the Quincy teachers, and later child-centered advocates built on these theoretical and practical ideas.

Social reconstructionists also found basic tenets for their positions among these writings. Foremost was the idea that everyone was endowed with the capacity to learn, and therefore, deserved an equal education. Comenius and Froebel taught the same curriculum to all classes, Wollstonecraft taught males and females together, and Douglass sought a just system without racial segregation. These steps toward inclusion were intended to break down society's artificial barriers to social justice in economic, social and political matters. Second, by including industrial and domestic arts in the curriculum, teachers made the curriculum immediately relevant to all students, challenging the mind/body distinction that had directed traditional schooling toward the powerful and pious. If students learned to reason and act with their heads, hands, and hearts in unison, all believed, then a more productive and harmonious society was likely to follow.

Many of Parker's (and later progressive educators') suggestions for reading education stemmed from these personal and social roots. Comenius advocated that students would learn to read more easily in their vernacular, working with topics of their immediate interest. Rousseau called for immersion in literacy practices and anticipated the transactional view of reading in his instructions to readers in *La Nouvelle Heloise*. Wollstonecraft recognized that content and genre matter in the development of serious readers and careful writers. Pestalozzi sought to coordinate reading and writing lessons and to embed them in the work of the communities. Froebel identified personal and social dialectics that would explain learners' authentic desire to become literate. Douglass demonstrated the social, cultural, and political work that reading and writing could do. In each argument, reading was intended to increase students' power and make them more agentive in their communities. Parker was modest and defensive but accurate when he declared, "I am simply trying to apply well-established principles of teaching" to the Quincy school board. He shared not only their pedagogical views but also their vision of reading education as the means to develop a more just society.

3

THE QUINCY METHOD IN CONTEXT

The old dame school disappeared at once. In place of it appeared something as different as light from darkness. The alphabet itself was no longer taught. In place of the old lymphatic, listless "schoolmarm," pressing into the minds of tired and listless children the mystic significance of certain hieroglyphics by mere force of overlaying, as it were – instead of this time-honored machine process – young women, full of life and nervous energy, found themselves surrounded at the blackboard with groups of little ones who were learning how to read in a word, exactly as they had before learned how to speak, not by rule or rote and by piecemeal, but altogether and by practice.

Charles F. Adams Jr.

In 1873, members of the Quincy School Committee broke with the tradition of teacher–directed oral examinations at the district's commencement activities in June. Rather than watch teachers and students perform the well-rehearsed program of questions, recitations, oral reading, and essay displays, committee members decided to ask their own questions of students. Although these questions covered similar content, they required students to reformulate the information and adapt the skills that they just performed so well. The students floundered badly under this questioning, particularly concerning their use of language. The committee's annual report concluded:

At present, as in the past, most of the pupils who finished the grammar course neither speak nor spell their own language very perfectly, nor read and write it with that elegance which is desirable. This immobility seems to show that a point has been reached which is near the natural term of such force as our present system of schooling is calculated to exert.

(Adams, 1879, p. 496)

The committee concluded that something had to change. Yet, because the cost of schooling had more than doubled since the end of the Civil War, and Quincy, like most of America, suffered under an economic recession, the committee hoped to accomplish the improvements while cutting the school budget. After a year of haggling, the committee decided to hire a superintendent to oversee the curriculum and expenses of Quincy's seven schools. Charles F. Adams, a local philanthropist and grandson of John Quincy Adams, would pay the salary (Campbell, 1965). After interviewing unemployed clergy, defeated politicians, and retired teachers, the committee chairman, John Quincy Adams, Jr., accepted the recommendation of a fishing partner to hire Francis Wayland Parker, a wounded war veteran, former teacher, and student of European educational philosophy. The contract required Parker's full-time commitment to improvement of Quincy schools and his assurance that he would move toward reform slowly.

On April 21, Parker met with Quincy teachers to explain his views of schooling and to organize the 42 teachers in order to study the science of education. Early the following week, Parker began demonstrating lessons in classrooms during and after school. Through these models and discussions, he invited teachers to rethink the organization of their schools and to reconsider how children learn. He required them to read Comenius, Pestalozzi, and Froebel; he integrated the subjects in the curriculum; and he shortened the school year. By all accounts, Quincy teachers responded quickly to these changes, starting with the ones Adams described in the quote opening this chapter. These early efforts became the celebrated "Quincy Method" and attracted an estimated 30,000 visitors to Quincy schools between 1876 and 1880.

Certainly, Parker deserves much of the credit for his part in the infectious spirit that enveloped Quincy teachers who offered students a different kind of education. Charles F. Adams demonstrated foresight and courage in supporting change, for hiring Parker, and for defending the Quincy Method annually at the school committee meeting. Yet at the time, it was clear to most that the teachers were the ones who made changes in curriculum and pedagogy possible. After the third year, only five of the original 17 primary teachers remained in Quincy employ because other districts had hired them to lead similar reforms. In fact, in Patridge's *The Quincy Method Illustrated,* teachers were acknowledged only by their initials in order to avoid such "poaching." "The method has now been four years in use in the schools of Quincy, and it has ceased to be an experiment, its advantages are questioned by none, least of all by teachers and parents" (Adams, 1879, p. 501).

The Quincy Method was based on four basic tenets. The first was the child's right to be him or her self; that is, to be happy in self initiated spontaneous activity that made sense for his or her stage of development. Parker elevated this proposition concerning individual freedom and authenticity to a social goal in much the same way Rousseau and Froebel had before him: "The end of all education should be to promote man's happiness, not only during his present transitory existence but throughout eternity which is to follow" (Parker, 1884, p. 1). The start of this harmonious existence was to be the primary classroom, in which students were to be responsible for what was done as well as for their levels of engagement and behavior.

Second, learning was considered to be natural, challenging, and enjoyable. Before Parker was hired, Quincy teachers acted as overseers and drillmasters, impressing abstract knowledge on students' minds according to rigid schedules and formal rules that defined and determined proper understanding and uses of that knowledge. Parker asked teachers to reconsider these assumptions. Adams described:

> Among the teachers are those who, having for years taught class after class in the old way, found themselves called upon to attempt with deep misgivings the new and to them mysterious process. They now join testimony to the others and confess that, to human beings, even though they be children, the ways of nature are the easier ways … . A child learns to talk and to walk without any instruction and by simple practice; the process of learning is not painful to the child or wearisome to others; on the contrary, it is an amusement to both.
>
> *(Adams, 1879, p. 501)*

In Quincy, students would acquire the abilities to read and write through its authentic use, and then, study the linguistic rules and cognitive strategies in order to talk about their literacies in a sophisticated manner.

Third, "the essence of the new system was that there was no system about it; it was marked throughout by intense individuality" (Adams, 1879, p. 500). Although basic principles were to be employed, uniformity among teachers was discouraged:

> The last new theory [the Lancaster system], so curiously, applied in some of our larger cities that vast numbers of children should be taught as trains and railroads are run, on timetable principles – that they are here now, that they will be at such another point tomorrow, and their terminus at such a date – while a general superintendent sits in his central office and pricks off each step in the advance of the whole line on a chart before him – this whole theory was emphatically "dismissed".
>
> *(p. 500)*

Quincy teachers used cautious experimentation to find that delicate balance among intervention, student initiative, and environmental impact in order to assure that both the "bright" and the "dull" students developed socially useful knowledge and skills.

Fourth, some Quincy teachers took up themes of social justice. Parker (1884) believed that traditional methods with abstract curriculum and teacher-centered pedagogy served "the aristocracy" rather than the masses. "The methods of the few, in their control of the many, still govern our public schools and to a great degree determine their management" (p. 436). Although Parker acknowledged that a standing army, religious institutions, and philanthropy tightened the aristocratic control, he maintained that traditional schooling was the primary means for social control because it sought to discipline each child's mind and body. Moreover, it served an ideological purpose, convincing the public that traditional schooling was the means to social, economic, and political advancement. "The problem [for the aristocrats] was to give the people education and keep them from exercising the divine gift of choice; to make them believe that they were educated and at the same time to prevent free action of the mind" (p. 408). Tying the fourth and first tenet together, Parker believed the science of education was "the one central means by which the great problem of human liberty is to be worked out" and "personal liberty is the one means of making the individual of worth to the mass" (Parker, 1902, p. 754).

These four tenets are apparent in Patridge's descriptions of lessons she observed during the year (1882) she spent with Quincy teachers. For example, Patridge described in detail a primary teacher's efforts to help her students inquire about the dignity of work by interviewing their families concerning the Quincy granite quarries – a major community business. In particular, the lessons focused on how employment influenced family life. Students gathered parents' perspectives in order to discuss and write about the stone, work, wages, and mothers' contributions to the family welfare. At the same time, an intermediate teacher invited her students to reconsider the Pilgrims' (and subsequent) treatment of Native Americans. This exchange to follow took place six years after the Battle of Little Big Horn and three years after the establishment of the Indian Training and Industrial School at Carlisle, PA.

> "We still have a few minutes left, let us talk more about the people whom we are going to study. Who are they, Henrietta?"
> "The Indians."
> "How long had they been in this country when the Puritans came?"
> "I don't know; I guess they always lived here."
> "Perhaps they did. No one knows certainly. When these white men landed in the Indian country, how did the Indians treat them?"
> "Kindly. They were good to them," is the unanimous opinion.
> "The children of the Puritans live here now; where are the children of the Indians?"
> "They've gone West!" "They've moved away!" are the vigorous answers; but the omnipresent slow boy, who sometimes says the right thing at the right time, takes his turn now and remarks in the most moderate and matter of fact fashion – "Those that they didn't kill, the white men drove away."
> "To whom did all this land belong before the white men came?"

"To the Indians," assent the entire class unhesitatingly.

"How did the Indians get their living?"

"By hunting and fishing!" is the general belief.

"Yes, and where did they hunt?"

"In the woods," is the ready reply.

"Children, the white men came here to the Indian's country, settled on his land, without paying him anything for it or even asking if they might have it. Cut down his forests to build their houses and keep their fields, shot the wild animals that live in these woods and often killed the Indians themselves; what do you think of that?"

This is such a sudden sally, coming from within their own gates too, that the young women and men look for a moment as if they were indeed involved in thought. But presently, Douglas finds an excuse and puts it thus: "Well, the Indians killed the white men" concluding triumphantly, "and took their scalps, too."

"That is true," grants the teacher, "but was it strange when the white men took everything away from the Indians and left them not even their land?"

"But this was a beautiful country and the white men wanted to come here to live," reasons a small sophist eagerly.

"So because they did, and because they knew more, and because there were more of them, and because they had guns, it was right for them to do it, was it?"

(Patridge, 1885, pp. 452–453)

The four tenets meant considerable changes to the literacy lessons as well. Formal grammar lessons were considered "a singularly unprofitable branch of instruction" (Adams, 1879, pp. 502–503). The textbooks were exchanged for reading "at sight" and writing "off hand."

The faculty of doing either one or the other of these could be acquired in only one way – by constant practice.... Instruction in reading, writing, grammar, spelling and to a very considerable degree in history and geography were combined in two exercises – reading and writing.

(p. 503)

The essence of Quincy lessons was to discover and develop functional uses of oral and written language in the daily lives of their community. "The process of learning to read, then, must consist of learning to use the written and printed word precisely as he used the spoken words" (Parker, 1883, p. 26).

In all the teaching and study of the art of teaching little children to read, that which aids directly in the act of association of words with their appropriate ideas aids the child in learning to read, and any other method, detail of

method or device that does not aid the mind in these acts hinders the child
in learning to read.

(pp. 27–28)

Function and meaning set the agenda for Quincy literacy lessons embedded in
students' study of the social and natural world. Students observed, drew, discussed, and labeled the events, practices, and things of their lives. "When the
child or group of children has been trained to observe attentively in nature, and
to talk fluently, the work of teaching reading may profitably be begun" (Parker,
1883, p. 78). To begin according to Patridge, Quincy teachers wrote the names
of objects of study on the blackboard, asking students what they wrote while
pointing at the object in question. After several students had pronounced the
word aloud, the teacher pronounced the word slowly in order to emphasize each
phoneme as they pointed to the corresponding spelling. Students followed this
example in chorus several times and then drew the letters of the word on their
slates while saying the word slowly. In this way, oral language directed the
learning of written language, with the relevance of reading and writing being
demonstrated and practiced continuously.

At the beginning of the third month of the first year, after studying farm
animals first hand, Mrs. L. walks to the board and begins to draw before a
group of seven.

"I guess you are going to make a picture for us?"

"I guess it's going to be a picture of a hen," ventures a bright-eyed little
girl, who hasn't taken her eyes from the drawing since it began.

"Oh! I know it's going to be a hen."

"Stanley?" [the teacher] calls, turning toward a row of last year's pupils,
who are sitting in their seats absorbed with some pasteboard animals, which
they are tracing on their slates. "I want you to help me, you are to be my
little teacher."

"Nellie, you may show the hen that is on the blackboard." Nellie points
to the picture.

"Now I am going to put another hen on the board for Stanley to find,
because you don't know this hen," writing "a hen" as she speaks.

Stanley puts his finger on it as soon as it's finished.

"What have you found Stanley?" inquires the teacher.

"A hen," briskly replies the boy.

The teacher writes "a hen" again on the board.

"Now Stanley and Nellie have each found a hen, and I want somebody
else to find one, Carrie?" selecting the brightest child.

The girl unhesitatingly points to the drawing.

"But that hen has been already found," protests the teacher. "Nellie show
it to us. You can see another, if you look," she adds encouragingly.

Carrie stands a moment and looks first at the drawing and then at the words, and finally, having apparently decided in her own mind that they mean the same thing, starts to put her finger on the nearest hen and then, probably remembering that Stanley had selected that one, she snatches her finger and places it on the word last written, turning with a quick smile of intelligence toward the teacher as she does so….

(Patridge, 1885, p. 52)

From the word to its letters and sounds, reading lessons moved regularly to the sentence level. These sentences were generated through oral questions in which students commented on, compared, and contrasted the object observed with others previously considered. These oral responses from students were transcribed on the blackboard and grammar, vocabulary, and spelling were discussed and practiced. During the first year, students would return to seats for "busywork" in which they made sentences around the words they had already considered and new words. In the second year, students started to "talk-with-a-pencil" independently. Parker (1883) advised teachers to "spend time in preparation for talking with the pencil. Training in talking with the tongue is one of the best ways of preparing for this work. If this be properly done, the words will drop off the pencil as easily and naturally as they drop off the tongue. Faith has a great deal to do with results" (p. 68). During the first three years of schooling, talking-with-a-pencil produced the primary texts for reading lessons.

During a Monday afternoon lesson at (Quincy's) Blackwell school, the teacher set two bean plants that the second year children planted several weeks before on the desk and asks, "What are these, Nellie?"

"Beans."

"Sadie?"

"Bean plants."

"What do you say children?"

"What is the difference between a bean and a bean plant, Willie?"

"One is nothing but a bean, and the other is a bean after it's been planted."

"Ada?"

[The class continues to describe and discuss the difference between beans and bean plants.]

"Just now I want to find out how much your eyes are worth," and taking her place behind the chair, she gently unwinds the tall vine from its stick, then using the latter for a spade, proceeds to dig up some of the plants, shake the earth from their roots, and lay them side by side on the top of the box. To complete this collection, which includes every stage of growth from the bean just sprouting to the plant with leaves, the teacher now adds a few swollen beans from the goblet of water on her desk. All being in readiness the children are invited to walk slowly – a line at a time – in front of the chair for a nearer view, then to pass on to their seats and begin to write what they have seen.

"Read us what you have written, Mary," commands the teacher, as the last little observer reaches his seat.

The child rises, slate in hand and reads – "Miss D took a sharp stick and dug up a bean."

"Sidney, what have you?"

"Now we call these bean plants," reads the boy.

"Yes, Luke?"

"The bean plant has roots."

(Patridge, 1885, pp. 221–223)

Parker's talking-with-a-pencil served three functions in Quincy schools: It was a second means for students to express themselves; it provided penmanship, spelling, and reading practice in a functional context; and it was the primary means through which teachers monitored students' development. As with all Quincy literacy activities, the teacher gradually released authority over the topics during the talking-with-a-pencil events. At first, teachers' or other students' questions stimulated the writing. In time, independent descriptions of behavior, pictures, or objects followed. After students demonstrated some facility with spelling and sentence structures, they began to write summaries of their reading, narratives about the day's events, and personal and fanciful stories. Patridge offered several examples of this development. These two are from beginning third-year students.

What I did this noon.

First I ate my dinner. Then I took my hat and got my bat and ball. Then I went out and began to play ball. Pretty soon I saw Greg and his brother. Greg had his whip. Charlie came over and said knock up flies. We did not play it, but we went up to see the bird's nest. There are four young ones in it. Charlie saw George and he asked him if he would play duck. He said, "No." But he did. I did not play. I went to school but I saw my Uncle Will. I asked him if he had the fish line. He did not answer. I asked him again. He said, "Come tonight and I'll give it to you."

The Pig Party.

One day as I was going down the road I met a pig and he was going for the woods. Now says I wherever there is one there is two and I follows the pig. And sure enough when I got in the woods I found four other pigs, one little one and three large ones. Now says I to myself I think I know whose pigs these are. And I went to the man's house who owned them and I told him. Then he gave me five cents, and I went and went[sic] and I bought a five cent top and string. When I went home I told my mother and she said very good.

(pp. 341–342)

After the annual evaluation of each student in 1878, Quincy School Committee chairman Adams wrote,

> I doubt if one in ten scholars knew what a noun, a pronoun, or an adjective was or could have parsed a sentence or explained the difference between its subject and its predicate. They could however put their ideas into sentences on paper with correctness and facility, and though they could not define what they were, they showed that they could use nouns, pronouns and adjectives in writing as well as they could in speech.... Out of five hundred grammar school children taken indiscriminately from all the schools, no less than four hundred showed results which were either excellent or satisfactory ... not only was there a marked improvement in attendance, but the attendance was cheerful. All this had been accomplished at reduced costs.
>
> *(pp. 503–504)*

Yet, despite quick successes, Parker's reforms were controversial. Working-class parents worried about the expense of the superintendent's salary, the lack of standards, and the apparent lack of discipline. Moreover, they worried that their children were being denied information they needed to improve their social and economic positions – the information that well-to-do children already knew. The school board kept the teachers' salaries low, which made it difficult for Parker to keep the ones that were producing the Quincy Method. Even Parker was only partially convinced that the methods were working. He considered the primary program "fairly a success" and the grammar school changes "by no means a failure" (as quoted in Campbell, 1965, p. 2). After being denied a raise or an appointment to the board of directors of the Adams Academy (a private preparatory high school for men considering college), Parker resigned in 1880 in order to accept a post as supervisor for Boston Public Schools. Three years later, he left that post to become director of the Cook County Normal School outside Chicago.

For a time, the Quincy Method flourished without Parker. In fact, Patridge observed classes after Parker left for Boston. Within the following decade, however, Adams resigned from the School Committee, 13 of the core elementary and grammar school teachers accepted employment in other school districts, and Parker's successor quit, declaring, "I would rather teach than serve in a slavish way the average School Committeeman" (as quoted in Campbell, 1965, p. 93). By the time physician Joseph Meyer Rice arrived in Quincy during his survey of American schools (1892), Quincy schools had retained none of Parker's teachers and the new faculty had abandoned the principles of a unified curriculum, teaching reading and writing as separate subjects once again. Rice found, however, that the "Quincy Method" had sprouted in nearly one third of the elementary schools across the country.

Portraits of the Public School System

> In some cities the schools have advanced so little that they may be regarded as representing a stage of civilization before the age of steam and electricity; in others, the people are just awakening to the fact that progress has been made in the spiritual as well as in the physical world; in still others, schools that have already advanced considerably along the line of progress may be found.... In our poorest primary schools the work is probably all formal, the pupils learning mechanically to read, write and cipher without acquiring any new ideas, while in our best primary schools the backbone of the work from the start is thought work, the pupil learning, in large par, to read and write and to a certain extent to cipher, while engaged in the acquisition of ideas.
>
> *(Rice, 1893, p. 114)*

Between January 7 and June 25, 1892, Rice sat in the classrooms of over twelve hundred teachers in 36 cities in Northeastern, Mid-Atlantic, and Midwestern states, taking copious notes, sketching examples, and testing students' reading, writing, and arithmetic. The results of his survey were serialized in *Forum Magazine*, creating concern among parents and educators alike. By the time the ninth instalment came to press, Rice's name "became a by-word, frequently an epithet, to school men across the nation" (Cremin, 1961, p. 4). Rice concluded:

> It is indeed incomprehensible that so many loving mothers whose greatest care appears to be the welfare of their children are willing without hesitation to resign the fate of their little ones to the tender mercies of ward politicians, who in many instances have no scruples in placing the children in classrooms the atmosphere of which is not fit for human beings to breathe and in the charge of teachers who treat them with a degree of severity that borders on barbarism.
>
> *(pp. 10–11)*

According to Cremin, Rice's critics were no less severe in their opinion of him and his study – "demonstrated beyond cavil that he is really a sensational critic" (*Boston Journal of Education*), "who recently abandoned the work of physicking his patients for a course in pedagogy in Germany" (*Education*) and "weak and inconsequential" (*School Journal*).

When Rice turned the *Forum* articles into a book (1893), he began to address his critics. He had studied psychology and pedagogy in Jena and Leipzig, Germany, for two years. His training as a pediatrician prepared him to evaluate the hygienic environment of classrooms and to make a "diagnosis of the standards of the schools" based on repeated observations of similar content and practices within and among schools. He cautioned the public to recognize that school documents are "political documents" meant to legitimize the policies in place, and he explained that corrupt school management was responsible for the deplorable state of American schools across much of the country. He asked his readers to remember "that school exists for the benefit of the child, and not for the benefit of boards of education, superintendents or teachers" (p. 4).

At the outset, Rice made a basic distinction between two types of school – the "old," "unscientific," and "mechanical" and the "new," "scientific," and "progressive." In the former, teachers still worked as overseers and drillmasters, attempting to transfer skills and facts from texts to students. In these classrooms, memory was prized above all else and perfect recitation was the criterion of evaluation. Rice concluded that this outdated philosophy of education offered little reason or incentive for teachers to study the academic content of the curriculum, pedagogical principles, or processes of learning because to this way of thinking, students (not their teachers) were responsible for mastery of the content and for its proper use. Reading and writing lessons and seatwork were systematically separated from content and were based on rote learning. Rice offered examples from classrooms in order to support his conclusions. In Baltimore,

> The reading was fully as mechanical as the arithmetic. It amounted simply to calling off words. Not only was there no expression, but there was not even an inflecting or pause at a comma or period. Nor did the teacher even correct mispronounced words, or make any attempt to teach the pupils how to read. Before the children began to read the designated lesson, there was a hideously mechanical introduction, including the calling off of the words placed at the top of the page, then, "Page 56, Lesson XVIII, The Dog and the Rat. Dog, Rat, Catch, Room, Run, Smell, Wag, Jump." And then came the story.
>
> *(p. 51)*

In Chicago,

> After entering the room containing the youngest pupils, the principal said to the teacher, "Begin with the mouth movements and go right through...." About fifty pupils now in concert give utterance to the sounds of a, e, and oo, varying their order, then a, e, oo, e a, oo, oo, a, e, etc. When some time had been spent in this maneuvering of the jaw, the teacher remarked, "Your tongues are not loose." Fifty pupils now put out their tongues and wagged them in all directions. The principal complimented the children on their wagging.
>
> *(pp. 176–177)*

Rice charged that four factors contributed to the poor state of most schools. Unconcerned parents followed traditions and did not acquaint themselves with issues of child development, scientific principles of learning, or the actual practices of schools. Meddling politicians appointed cronies as superintendents, principals, and teachers and tampered with school budgets. Uninformed and overworked supervisors upheld the status quo. And overconfident teachers thought they had nothing to learn about the curriculum, teaching, or learning and were content with their practices. Rice did not mince words: "The real causes for the existence of the mechanical schools at the present stage of civilization are no other than corruption and selfishness on the part of school officials, and unjustifiable ignorance as well as criminal negligence, on the parts of parents" (p. 26).

According to Rice, new, scientific, and progressive education was designed to help students develop their abilities to observe and reason so that they might apply their new knowledge and skills in meaningful social contexts. Teachers were to provide environments "to develop the child naturally in all his facilities – intellectual, moral, and physical" (p. 21). Within this environment teachers observed students' actions, words, and artifacts closely in order to determine their stage of development and their particular instructional needs. These observations enabled teachers to develop and adapt curricula accordingly and to intervene in students' processes of developing understandings for the topics and the attendant practices. In this way, both the student and the teacher became responsible for student learning. By accepting this responsibility, teachers acknowledged that they had much to learn in and about their work. New forms of teacher preparation and professional development were needed. Rice reported: "as my remarks will show, by far the most progress has been made in those cities where the teachers themselves are the most earnest students" (p. 18).

Rice visited only 10 school districts that approximated this ideal of new education. He divided these 10 into two groups – seven in transition from old to new and three in an advanced state of new development. Rice argued that schools' commitment to principles of a unified curriculum separated the districts. All 10 districts had teachers using observation for curriculum development and lesson planning. Each had divorced itself from politics and hired school officials based on educational philosophy. All had changed discipline policies, loosening the reins on students' bodies as well as their minds. Yet only three had taken the step to embed reading and writing instruction within the study of society and nature. Rather in seven of the districts, reading and writing were taught as separate subject areas apart from rich stories or interesting information. Rice argued that without unification, students would not see the social utility of reading and writing, and, moreover, they would not see the natural connections among school subjects and their utility in everyday problem solving.

At the time of his visit, St. Paul, Minnesota schools were in this state of transition. "My visits to the St. Paul schools were made just fifteen months after the inauguration of the new board, and already at that time there was unmistakable evidence that the schools were rapidly improving" (p. 184). Political appointments had subsided, and teachers' education had begun. Additional supervisors had been hired to help teachers in their transition to the new philosophy of education. Kindergartens opened in all elementary and grammar schools; manual training was added to the elementary grades; and schools reached out to their communities. Yet, "a year and a half is a short time for improving a school system ... the relics of the old system were at the time of my visit still visible in some schools" (p. 186). Most noticeable was that reading and writing were still separated as subjects in many schools. Although jaw maneuvers and tongue loosening were not observed as they had been in Chicago, word lists, spelling bees, and reciting from primer and reader stories were often apparent. Overall however, Rice concluded that progress would continue because school officials and teachers were reaching out to their communities.

> A short time before Thanksgiving Day, a number of teachers, acting on their own behalf, asked the pupils to contribute a share, however small, toward rendering Thanksgiving Day happy for the poor.... On the following day every pupil who had been present brought something to school each according to his means. Indeed, so many things were brought that the question of storing them became a difficult problem. Before long, the news reached the ears of every teacher in the city. The result was that nearly every school child in St. Paul contributed something ... more than enough had been given by children to supply all the poor of St. Paul with food and clothing for the winter.
>
> *(p. 192)*

According to Rice, schools in Minneapolis, LaPorte (Indiana), and Cook County (Illinois) provided the most scientific schooling in America. Although they would continue to develop, he assumed, teachers in these schools worked actively toward the unification of reading and writing with the systematic study of science, geography, literature, and the arts without detriment to basic skills. "Instruction in almost every branch [of the curriculum] partakes of the nature of a language lesson, the child being led to learn the various phases of language in large part incidentally while acquiring and expressing ideas" (p. 223); "while gaining ideas from written or printed page, they are learning how to read" (p. 223); and "while thus rendering their ideas more clear, they learn spelling, penmanship, the construction of sentences, and how to write compositions" (p. 224). In these schools, Rousseau's "curse of childhood" reading lessons were eliminated "and school life was from the beginning made fascinating" (p. 224).

In order to make this last point clear, Rice contrasted the mechanical schools with those in transitional and advanced stages. For example, he focused on discipline as the main contrast between St. Louis and LaPorte. St. Louis teachers continued to make students literally toe the mark in order to learn, admonishing students as they stood in line to recite their lessons, "How can you learn anything with your knees and toes out of order" (p. 98). In contrast, during the LaPorte's Principal's Club the superintendent asked teachers for "consideration for the child, sympathy" when considering how students might demonstrate what they have learned at school. Rice explained, "The [LaPorte] teacher uses every means at her command to render the life of the child happy and beautiful, while learning" (p. 101). Rice pointed toward differing teacher qualifications between Chicago and St. Paul: "The qualifications required for passing the teachers' examination in Chicago were not much, if any, beyond those possessed by one who attended a high school for one year." In St. Paul, however, "In April, semi-weekly classes for the study of plants were organized in different parts of the city, under the auspices of the St. Paul Teachers' Association, and attended by from one hundred and fifty to two hundred teachers." Science was to be unified with reading and writing instruction during the following year.

Toward the end of his travels for his survey, Rice returned to Minneapolis, LaPorte, and Cook County in order to gather more examples of results of scientific reading instruction; to show the diversity among the new scientific approaches; and to test third-year students in reading, writing, and arithmetic in order to document uniformity in results. In an addendum to his book, he shared the special features of each district. In Minneapolis as in the other two, he found schools that treated teachers as learners, unified curriculum, and enlightened discipline. He highlighted the outcomes for low-income immigrant students "who knew very little if anything of the English language when they are first sent to school" (p. 256). After inspecting essays and listening to students read aloud, he concluded that after two years all traces of difference in written language facility had vanished because he was unable to identify systematic differences between local and immigrant students' work. However, he assured his readers and demonstrated that he could easily determine which essays came from Minneapolis schools and which from mechanical schools in other cities:

> The schools offer, in my opinion, positive proof to the effect that when teachers are competent it is entirely unnecessary for them to resort to unusual measures in a school attended by a poor class of foreigners, either in regard to discipline or to the methods employed in teaching the English language".
>
> *(p. 257)*

In LaPorte, Rice concentrated on the artistic talents of the students and on the cooperative and social interests of students as they worked. LaPorte teachers had worked toward a unified curriculum (science and literacy) for 10 years prior to Rice's visit. With only 30 teachers in the district, faculty development proved much easier than in the larger districts and consistency among teachers and across schools was apparent. Visual arts were central to the LaPorte curriculum. Starting in the first year with pencil, brush, and clay, LaPorte students sketched, painted, and constructed natural and societal environments at levels that Rice found comparable to students in upper elementary grades from other districts. To foster conversations and to share teaching responsibilities, LaPorte teachers encouraged students to work cooperatively on most curricular projects. For example, first-year students observed natural phenomena in teams, taking collective notes and collaborating on visual representations of what they observed. Fifth-year students produced cooperative interdisciplinary projects in geography, literature and science. Rice noted that LaPorte classrooms were arranged accordingly. Small square tables with four chairs replaced the rows of bolted desks. As Cuban (1984) attested, this type of arrangement was not commonplace in classrooms until the 1960s in most parts of the country.

Rice saved his most lavish praise for Cook County: "of all the schools that I have seen, I know of none that shows so clearly what is implied by an educational ideal as the Cook County Normal School" (p. 210). Francis Parker had been the director at Cook County for 10 years prior to the visit and had attracted exceptional teachers to the schools. One teacher, Walter Jackman, had inspired the ideal of curricular unification through his design of a science and language program. The curriculum unfolded on a 20-acre campus with student-maintained gardens, several ponds, a zoological garden, and a museum. Students studied botany, zoology, physics, chemistry, and geology in all grades and developed scientific literacy by studying and producing texts on these subjects. According to Rice, student texts rivaled professional quality in some cases and even the primary grade students' work outshone those of high school students from mechanical schools.

After his second visit to the advanced, scientific schools, Rice was unequivocal about the superiority of the basic skills demonstrated in progressive schools.

> And strange as it may seem, it is nevertheless true that the results in reading and in the expression of ideas in writing are, at least in the primary grades, by far the best in schools where language in all its phases is taught incidentally, and poorest in the schools that devote time to mechanical reading and writing.
>
> *(p. 224)*

His test of students' reading included oral reading and a discussion of the passage read – third-year students were asked to read at sight from a previously unseen text and were then evaluated according to their fluency, expression, accuracy, and ability to summarize. In Rice's judgment, students in new schools ranged from fair to excellent, with the "majority of pupils reading ... as might be expected of any one" (p. 234). For writing, Rice collected first draft samples on topics of student choice from 7,000 students and compared them on content, function, and form. He concluded that students learning in a unified curriculum were not any less competent in the use of standard English than those who studied spelling and grammar separately and that they were far superior in terms of the presentation of content and sense of audience. With these test results, Rice thought the debate over methods of teaching reading and writing was over. "It is frequently claimed in support of the mechanical system that the old education is more practical than the new. This assertion, however, is made in ignorance of the facts" (p. 23).

To put Rice's assessment of American schools in some historical perspective it is important to recognize the power of the word *science* in the newly emerging field of education. Post-Darwinian conceptions of science were disrupting most traditional ways of understanding nature and society. For Parker and Rice, this meant that teachers' close systematic and intentional observation of children in order to discern patterns of intellectual, emotional, and social development (child study) should replace religious tenets or historical precedent in decisions concerning curriculum and pedagogy. They were progressive in their outlook and sensitive to the capabilities of previously marginalized groups – as were the teachers they encouraged. At that time, child study competed on an equal basis with the beginnings of experimentation and precise measurement (to become scientific management) in order to explain human psychology (Lagemann, 2000). However, the same year that Rice published his book (1893), the National Education Association (NEA) summoned college presidents, faculty, and two school superintendents under the direction of US Commission of Education William Torrey Harris to revise the high school curriculum toward college entrance standards. *The Committee of Ten Report* proposed that all students be taught mathematics, geography, history, grammar, sciences, languages, literature, and the arts in the same way as long as they remained in school. *The Report* challenged teachers to engage and encourage students, cultivating their minds and teaching them to think.

At Francis Parker's request, the NEA charged a committee to recommend reforms for the elementary schools. In 1895 under Harris's direction, *The Committee of Fifteen Report* called for a junior version of the high school curriculum – complete with charts of separate subject and minutes of study per week. Both reports ignored child study and Parker's and Rice's recommendations, banking on more rigorous changes to the traditional curriculum rather than smarter, more sensitive teachers to meet the challenges of industrialization, urbanization, and immigration. Rice would eventually shift his views about science in education, publishing his second education tome *The Scientific Management of Education* in 1912. In 1899, Francis Parker was dismissed from Cook County Normal School because of parental concerns and retreated to the Chicago Institute (later the University of Chicago School of Education) where he met John Dewey.

4

JOHN DEWEY AND THE SCHOOLS OF TOMORROW

It remains but to organize all the factors to appreciate them in their fullness of meaning, and to put the ideas and ideals involved into complete, uncompromising possession of our school system. To do this means to make each one of our schools an embryonic community, active with types of occupations that reflect the life of the larger society, and permeated throughout with the spirit of art, history, and science. When the school introduces and trains each child of society into membership within such a little community saturating him with the spirit of service, and then providing him with the instruments of effective self-direction, we shall have the deepest and best guarantee of a larger society which is worthy, lovely, and harmonious.

John Dewey

When John Dewey accepted the position as head of the Department of Philosophy, Psychology, and Pedagogy at the newly founded University of Chicago in 1894, he enrolled his son, Fred, in Miss Flora Cooke's class at the Cook County Normal Elementary School. His daughter, Evelyn, started there the following year. By all accounts, the Deweys were satisfied with and often laudatory toward the school's curriculum and Miss Cooke's pedagogy in particular. However, when Dewey began his school experiment at the University of Chicago in 1896, Fred and Evelyn transferred to the new school. Dewey's *School and Society* (1899), the first book about his school, was the result of three lectures offered to the parents of the first cohort to enrol. In these lectures, he summarized what he meant by the school's role in the development of a worthy, lovely, and harmonious society.

Dewey's Vision for Education

Dewey considered philosophy to be the primary means through which people could understand the social, political and moral dimensions of their lives. To render philosophy practical, Dewey accepted the idea that philosophy was made less out of intellectual abstractions than it was developed from social and emotional experiences. In order to understand themselves, others, and the world around them, people should dig deeply into their everyday experiences in light of the historical circumstances that shape and are shaped by those experiences. At that time, this meant working to understand how the application of science to industrial production through capitalism was influencing people's everyday lives and understandings. To make this application, American industry summoned workers from rural areas and across international borders, changing their routines, commitments, and dispositions in order to fit a factory system. Traditional forms of education, and even schooling, had not prepared workers and their families for these changes.

In the new urban environment, industry and commerce replaced the household as the center of the productive economy. The production of clothing, tools, furniture, and even food became separated from most Americans' lives. Production work was divided into repeated actions ruled by the clock. Exchange became a financial transaction. Institutions and community life were reorganized to accommodate these new processes and to discipline the lives of workers of all ages in order to maximize effectiveness, efficiency, and profits. In return, workers were freed from traditional ties to place and family and freed to choose where to work and what to buy among the new goods that they and others produced. Dewey noted the difficulty that many workers and families experienced and concluded this transaction was particularly puzzling for the young because they lost the "habits of industry, order, and regard for the rights and ideas of others, and the fundamental habit of subordinating their activities to the general interest of the household" (Dewey, 1899, p. 24). This loss of bearings, he argued, threatened social cohesion and distorted the possibilities of democracy.

In his search for philosophical solutions, Dewey began with the observation that social classes experienced this fragmentation of life differently. He accused the upper classes of using democracy as propaganda to better their circumstances. "In the name of democracy and individual freedom, the few as a result of superior possessions and powers had in fact made it impossible for the masses of men to realize personal capacities and to count in the social order" (Dewey & Tufts, 1908, p. 443). Existing laws, policies and institutions, he charged, had been "harnessed to the dollar" – designed to maximize profits at the expense of peoples' abilities to participate actively and equally in civic life. He concluded "that until there is something like economic security and economic democracy, aesthetic, intellectual, and social concerns will be subordinated to an exploitation by the owning class which carries with it the commercialization of culture" (Dewey, 1928, p. 270).

True democracy, Dewey countered, must be far more than a form of government or an expression of popular sovereignty. It should be an associated method of living together that breaks down barriers between people (Dewey, 1901). A true democracy would produce ways of living in which the means for self-realization were embedded within the realization of all others in a community (Dewey, 1891) and would meet the needs of all through "free and mutual harmonizing of different individuals with every person sharing in the determination of the conditions and aims of his own work" (Dewey, 1910, p. 268). Dewey argued that the maldistribution of wealth in America was the primary barrier to a true democracy. "If democracy is to achieve the higher and more complete unity for every single human being, it can fulfill that destiny only by substituting economic democracy for the existing economic aristocracy" (Dewey, 1888, p. 26). In order to make that substitution, citizens would need to exchange their dysfunctional, traditional static social knowledge for a more dynamic, pragmatic social knowledge of true democracy. Education could be a catalyst for that exchange. "Democracy has to be born anew every generation, and education is the midwife" (Dewey, 1916, p. 83).

In this way, Dewey sought to address two questions: how can we organize schooling to reflect the changing social context – to align schooling with industrial society – and how can we ensure that this reorganization builds upon and aligns with democratic ideals.

> We want change, variety, growth, and the ability to grow requiring the conscious effort of intelligence and the active direction of will, and this can be given only upon condition that the automatic mechanism of the soul attends to all demands made habit.
>
> *(Dewey, 1891a, p. 115)*

For Dewey, an individual's understanding of her needs directed her conscious efforts of intelligence or the acquisition of knowledge. This functional view of thinking allows ideas to be considered tentative plans of action set to address real problems. Dewey charged that traditional schooling was organized to transmit to and then to judge students by their capacities to digest crystalized knowledge and, therefore, it could not prepare students to understand and address the existing challenges of rapid social change. Only a new schooling, he hypothesized, could prepare students with the fluid social knowledge necessary to address changes present and those to come. "Everyone must have his fitness judged by the whole, including the anticipated change, not merely by reference to the conditions of today, because these may be gone tomorrow" (Dewey, 1898, p. 328).

His challenge to educators was to provide experiences that allowed students to form intellectual, social and emotional habits but prevented the habits from becoming so fixed that they became dysfunctional with even modest social change. "Habits are and must be so manipulated that they remain cooperating factors in the conscious reconstruction of experience for human betterment" (Dewey, 1922, p. 37). Students, he reasoned, would continuously remake true democracy by engaging and reflecting on these more basic, simplified levels of this ideal. In a sense, Dewey was adapting Rousseau's concept of a nonsocial (negative) education, one that simultaneously contradicted society at large in order to inform/reform that society currently and in the future. This tension was at the heart of his philosophy of education captured in the concepts from the quote that began this chapter – "fullness of meaning," "embryonic community," "occupations," "saturating," "self-direction," "spirit of service," "worthy, lovely, and harmonious."

Because Dewey's philosophy on democracy, learning, and education took the form of tentative hypotheses provoked by the breakdown of social traditions during industrialization (urbanization and immigration), he was obliged according to his pragmatism to test them against experience. In January 1896, with the help of many others, he organized an experimental school with 16 pupils and two teachers. During the seven years of existence, the school occupied three different buildings, grew to 140 students, and employed 23 teachers and 10 part-time assistants.

The Laboratory School

It is not the purpose, as had been stated, of this school that the child learn to bake, and sew at school, and to read, write, and figure at home. It is true, however, that these subjects of reading, writing, etc. are not presented during the early years in large doses. Instead, the child is led by other means to feel the motives for acquiring skill in the use of these symbols, motives which persist when competition, often the only motive in the early years in many schools, ceases. In this school, as well as in all schools, if a child realizes the motive for acquiring a skill, he is helped in large measure to secure the skill. Books and the ability to read are, therefore, regarded strictly as tools. The child must learn to use these, just as he would any other tool.

(Dewey, 1897, p. 72)

According to Katherine Camp Mayhew and Anna Camp Edwards, two of the early teachers at the Laboratory School and later its most able chroniclers (1936), the school experienced three distinct phases. The first, which they characterized as more error than trial, lasted six months. At its end, the school was completely reorganized. The school's second stage consisted of two years of calculated and unending experimentation in curriculum, organization, administration, and instruction. This was followed by a five-year third phase of refinement and extension. By design, the school was community-centered, not child-centered, throughout its phases (Dewey, 1936a). Students, teachers, and parents were considered community members who planned the programs and curriculum together in order to "harmonize" the children's interests and lives with adult ends and values. Projects began from children's interests and teachers were to help them connect those interests to matters of the world outside the home and classroom through principles of language, science, and social studies. In order to promote cooperation, all activities were collective. The teachers' role was to guide children in developing plans for action, to observe and mediate students' engagements, and to recognize signs of intellectual and social growth.

For example, when seven- and eight-year-olds declared an interest in weaving, the teachers helped them to reach back to different methods of spinning and weaving in the American colonial period. "They learned that the invention of machines had brought many improved ways of living, had changed the organization pattern of many industries, and had left many industrial and social problems for later generations to solve" (Mayhew & Edwards, 1936, p. 194). Teams of students built a loom, interviewed immigrant weavers from the surrounding community, and began to consult books to determine how weaving was conducted in different parts of the world. The project harnessed and extended their knowledge of physics, design, literacy, history, geography, mathematics, and art, engaging their bodies, minds, and emotions simultaneously.

> The children realized somewhat the position of the spinner and weaver, the beginnings of organization in several branches of the industry, the mis-understandings of the value of machines and the benefit of machine work to the community, and the riots which followed any invention replacing hand-work.
>
> *(p. 194)*

Although the projects were expected to have "a positive content and intrinsic value of their own, which call forth the inquiry and constructive attitude on the part of the pupil" (Dewey, 1897, p. 47), teachers were faced each day – each hour – with the task of making connections to the community and identifying critical moments of potential growth when an experience could be/should be extended. These demands required two types of ongoing professional development. Content knowledge and its connections were addressed by dividing the faculty into departments for which individuals became responsible for developing expertise. The authorities, then, would assist teachers and students in the development of factual and conceptual knowledge within disciplines and topics. The assessment knowledge was developed in weekly meetings in which teachers discussed and theorized actual student cases from the artifacts they had produced. Content knowledge expertise drew from community members, business leaders, and residents from Jane Addams' Hull House. The pedagogical and assessment discussions brought professors from the University of Chicago to consult and to learn. All were involved in continuous discussions of what types of individuals, which values, and what actions the school intended to develop.

Teachers worked from a general stage theory of student interest and capabilities. Four- to six-year-olds engaged in social activities that elicited physical activity, emotional attachment, and verbal discussions of events. Seven- to ten-year-olds displayed more sophistication in their consideration of activities and paid more attention to the symbolic representations of their thoughts and deeds. Eleven- to fifteen-year-olds sharpened their use and analyses of interests and talents and directed their interests more responsibility through sophisticated investigation, reflection, and generalization. Within and among these stages, teachers watched for authentic opportunities to introduce literacy and genuine signs of student interest. Mayhew and Edwards acknowledged explicitly that parents and teachers feared violating traditional roads to the alphabet, jumping at chances to teach.

> This is often taken by the inexperienced teachers as an indication that [the student] has arrived at the stage of growth where the use of this tool arises out of a genuine need. An observant teacher, however, will recognize this as premature, if in other situations the child gives evidence of immaturity.
>
> *(p. 380)*

The test for teachers was to determine if the child considered learning to read and write as ends in themselves (premature) or if they recognized what reading was for and what writing could do (genuine). The Laboratory School teachers observed students in all activities to judge their interest. If they continued to play at the characters involved in the projects – pretend to be a carpenter – teachers would refrain from introducing reading and writing formally. If however, the students would plan their actions according to the social roles of the agent – gather tools thoughtfully according to the group's intentions, draw diagrams, or rehearse lists of actions to be taken when building – then formal instruction could begin with the likely prospect of rapid success. Because the processes of mental development were considered to be social processes internalized through partici-pation, teachers understood children's recognition of the utility of literacy to be gradual and embedded in experience. Accordingly, teachers took active, but not aggressive, roles in children's development of genuine interest in literacy.

For example, all students were expected to keep daily records of their progress toward the goals of their projects. This practice took place at the end of the morning or day depending on the time invested. The youngest students observed the older using their literacy skills to make their notes, and they were expected to dictate their report to teachers who would translate verbatim on their sheets as they talked with the child about the correct form, clarity, and accuracy. Regardless of the student's age or facility, "the child became conscious of the structure of the sentence, of the place of and use of modifying words in phrases, and of the position of the latter in the sentence and of the need to use paragraph form" (Mayhew & Edwards, 1936, p. 338). Modeling of literacy in these ways across the day, weeks, and years afforded both younger and older students opportunities to recognize and refine their understanding of the value of literacy as a tool.

> The desire to read for themselves was often born in children out of the idea that they might find better ways of doing and thus, get more satisfactory results. With this interest as an urge, the child himself often freely sets his attention to learning to read. A rational need thus became the stimulus to the gaining of skill in the use of a tool.
>
> *(p. 381)*

Beyond demonstrations of the utility of literacy in projects, student records and the practices of their production provided students with opportunities to participate in the continuous negotiations of the school life and governance. The reports became records of progress toward goals inviting assessments of past decisions and suggestions for new choices. Each student participated in these practices and their written accounts were available to others even when the authors/students were not present. This daily practice developed habitual use of descriptive and interpretive language, requiring comments concerning both means and ends of their daily work. As artifacts, the records represented the work accomplished and could serve as evidence about whether the group's original hypotheses for action were accurate or in need of adjustment in order to reach their goals. These practices of testing thought against experience, while being reflexive about goals and actions, provided every student with the simplified, protected environments in which they could learn to think and act toward a true democracy.

Once students demonstrated a genuine interest in learning to read and write, they were assigned to a teacher who specialized in techniques of reading and writing. Although the lessons were always meaning-oriented, teachers became much more explicit about alphabetic principles, grammatical structures, and usage. During the second stage of development (seven- to ten-year-olds), the lessons were part of expressive arts, occupying two and one half hours per week in the curriculum. Most often the students read and wrote stories, poems, songs and personal narratives, introducing them to aesthetic, cultural, and emotional reasons for reading and writing. For older students (third stage, 11–15 years), the school day was not segmented into formal lessons. Rather projects required different types of reading and writing in order to serve students' needs for gathering information and representing what they were learning. Although the school environment included the neighborhood, school grounds, shops, and classrooms, the school library was at the center of the Laboratory School – filled with texts from all walks of life, the many cultures represented in the community, and the students' artifacts.

Wynne Laskerstein, a literacy specialist teacher, recalled experiences of lessons from the opening and experimental phases of the school.

> The materials which were chosen for their reading lessons were taken chiefly from their history [lessons], with occasional change to other subjects, shopwork or cooking. It soon became evident that their power to give a definite account of their work and their interest in doing it were in direct ratio to the degree of activity involved in the original lessons. It was often impossible to obtain a clear statement of their history, even on the day in which it had been presented to them and frequently different members of the group would give contradictory statements with regard to the most essential point. But whenever hand work was the subject of discussion, they recalled with comparative ease the desired details.

A notably successful lesson was the result of a talk about the making of their loom. Sentences were put on the blackboard by the teacher as the children gave them and were read and reread by the class. A list made of the new words, chiefly the names of tools, and a drill upon these was given by acting out the uses of the various tools. Individual children were chosen to direct the action by pointing to certain words or to find on the blackboard the name of the tool that others were using. The children were delighted and spent the entire period at the blackboard without fatigue. They called this writing "putting the tools in the shop," and one boy insisted upon buying each tool from the teacher before he wrote its name, gravely pro-offering imaginary money and insisting that the tool be wrapped up in paper and duly delivered.

(as quoted in Mayhew & Edwards, 1936, pp. 350–351)

Georgia Brown (1900) provided an account of a reading and writing lesson for nine-year-olds.

A period was given to finishing their written stories and one to reading them aloud. This exercise gave an opportunity for a review of the work on the Plymouth colony in which the children were asked questions suggested by their papers. Later each child chose some topic from the story of the Pilgrims. One began at the beginning; another chose the first encounter, and some could choose without help. The papers were much better than those that they had composed as a group by dictating to the teacher and then copying from the blackboard. The children worked much more industriously, tired of their work less quickly, and showed greater freedom of expression. The work was continued through a second period at their own request.

(p. 79)

For the younger students, these literacy lessons touched upon the domestic and industrial arts and the scientific knowledge of historic periods. Their literacy enabled students to develop insights in the moral, political and social issues of the periods and fueled their imaginations when they attempted to relive the lives of the people they studied. In this way, students' reading and writing contributed meaningfully to the development of the social knowledge upon which their contemporary community structures were built.

The seven-year history of the Laboratory School lasted just long enough for its first cohort to progress through all its grades. Its experimental methods of teaching reading and writing were therefore not completely tested. However, the self-directed demands on literacy were quite high for students in the third stage of development. Along with record keeping and formal study of English, these students wrote and printed a geometry textbook (based on construction of a building), read and performed Greek tragedies and Shakespearian plays (for the community), read and translated Caesar's *Commentaries* from Latin, and formed a debating society. Teachers, parents, and Dewey accepted performance of these tasks and the production of the artifacts of the projects as evidence that new approaches to learning to read and write produced equal, if not superior, results of accuracy, fluency, and interest to the traditional methods. All were convinced that the Laboratory School student developed much more sophisticated under-standings of what reading is for and what writing can do and demonstrated that knowledge in addressing community problems.

Of course, the methods were not completely successful for every student. "I never learned to spell. I do not know how to spell now [30 years later]. I have not any sense of spelling.... I do not remember any studying or learning of anything. I don't remember going through the process of learning to read, but I read" (Paul McClintock 1930, as quoted in Mayhew & Edwards, 1936, pp. 404–405). But for most students, the experiences at the Laboratory School allowed them to develop a self-conscious, self-directed, reflexive understanding of reading and writing.

> As the years have passed and as I have watched the lives of many Dewey School children, I have been astonished at the ease which fits them into all sorts of conditions of emergencies; they go ahead and work out the problems at hand, guided by their positively formed working habits.
>
> *(Helen Greeley, as quoted in Mayhew & Edwards, 1936, p. 406)*

Schools of Tomorrow

After its seventh year, the president of the University of Chicago proposed a merger between the Laboratory School and the late Francis Parker's Chicago Institute under Dewey's direction from the university's newly formed Depart-ment of Education. A dispute over the retention of the Laboratory School's faculty and staff led Dewey to resign the new school's directorship after one year. During a salary disagreement with the university, Dewey accepted a position at Columbia University in 1905 where he remained for the rest of his academic career. While writing his major educational work, *Democracy and Education* (1916), Dewey collaborated with his daughter Evelyn in a survey of schools attempting the new "progressive" education. Roughly twenty years had passed since Rice completed his survey. She traveled among the schools and returned to New York with artifacts and notes for analysis and explanation. The work was published as *Schools of Tomorrow* (1915).

The book begins with a discussion of Marietta Johnson's Organic School in Fairhope, Alabama. Established in 1907 with a benefactor's promise to contribute $25 monthly for its budget, Johnson tested Rousseau's primary educational hypothesis – "the child is best prepared for life as an adult by experiencing in childhood what has meaning to him as a child, and further, the child has a right to enjoy his childhood" (Dewey & Dewey, 1915, pp. 17–18). Having been established in a single tax county, the Organic School had a political side as well, following Henry George's advocacy for social justice through community ownership of public services. In her own account of the school, Johnson (1929) argued: "every problem which now confronts civilization will be solved eventually only by education.... A fully developed individual earnestly seeks to understand the rights of others, and is keenly interested to see that fundamental justice prevails" (p. 15).

Johnson adapted a group-form of Rousseau's "negative education," keeping young children away from reading and writing in order to shield them from too early exposure to adult foibles and vicarious experience. At the Organic School, young children pursued an unspecified curriculum based on physical exercise, nature study, music, handwork, field geography, storytelling, sense culture, fundamental concepts of number, dramatization, and games. They were to follow their interests without assigned lessons, examination, grading or failures. "There is no fixed curriculum, but the teachers keep a simple record of work done as a guide to the next teacher" (Johnson, 1938, p. 70). This reliance on experience was intended to develop students as critical thinkers with "the ability to wait for data, to hold the mind open and ready, to receive new facts, to delay decisions and opinions" (Johnson, 1929, p. 128). For each student, reading and writing would come in their time.

> Because the young child is unfitted by reason of his soft muscles and his immature senses to the hard task of setting down to fine work on the details of things, he should not begin school by learning to read and write, nor by learning to handle small playthings or tools.
>
> *(Marietta Johnson, as quoted in Dewey & Dewey, 1915, p. 21)*

> The pupils are not allowed to use books until the eighth or ninth year, and by this time they have realized so keenly their need, they beg for learning. The long tiresome drill necessary for six-year-old children is eliminated. Each child is anxious to read some particular book, so there is little or no need to trap his attention, or to insist on an endless repetition.
>
> *(p. 36)*

> A young teacher taught a class of eight-year-old children to read. She offered them work which had been outlined for six-year-olds and found that they were able to do a week's work in one day and a month's work in a week. They were so eager, her only fear was that they might overdo.
>
> *(Johnson, 1938, p. 11)*

> Mrs. Johnson is convinced that a child who does not learn to read and write in her school until he is ten years old, is as well read at fourteen and writes

and spells as well as a child of fourteen in a school where the usual curriculum is followed.

(Dewey & Dewey, 1915, p. 36)

The Deweys reported discussions of sophisticated text among the Organic School students, commenting in some detail on the reading and dramatizing of Greek myths, the *Iliad*, and the *Odyssey*. Through these discussions, teachers attempted to connect the plots, ideas, and emotions of the past with the students' present experiences, demonstrating how texts are interpretations of social interactions and their consequences. Johnson understood literacy as agency and she intended to develop students' literacy to a point at which they would work to improve a society based currently on "ignorance, indifference, and contempt for human rights" (Johnson, 1929, p. 15).

Schools of Tomorrow focused primarily on urban schools, showing that teachers continued to develop progressive means of teaching reading and writing as tools. At the laboratory school near the University of Missouri, they noted that "pupils learn to read and write and figure only as they felt the need of it to enlarge their work … about trees, plants and animals or to study their own food, shelter, and clothing" (pp. 44–45). "In Chicago, English is not taught as a separate subject to the younger grades, but the pupils have compositions to write for their history lessons, and they keep records of their excursions and other work" (p. 85). In Public School No. 26 in Indianapolis, "located in the poor, crowded, colored district of the city, the school has a branch library and pupils and community neighbors are taught how to use it" (pp. 220–221).

After the preliminary analyses of schools of tomorrow, Evelyn Dewey returned to Porter, Missouri in order to develop an in-depth case study of a progressive, community-centered rural school within a community experiencing economic and social stagnation because of industrialization and urbanization. She published her results in *New Schools for Old* (1919). Before the school intervened, Porter farmers held "general contempt for book farming, making them refuse to listen to advice from agricultural colleges and stations and leaving them wholly at a loss in dealing with a new problem" (p. 17). The community was losing it social capital as well, community clubs and organizations were in decline, farmers and their wives were isolated on their farms, and the community infrastructure was sadly neglected. A small group of community members contacted a nearby teachers college to hire a new schoolteacher with progressive ideas. Under the new direction of Marie Turner Harvey, the school was organized "to raise the standards of efficiency to the point where problems can be settled by a body of intelligent, prosperous, and progressive farmers" (p. 2). According to Dewey, "If the school is working with a definite aim and with social ideals, the immediate influence of the school on the whole community is easily traced" (p. 19).

Dewey began her trace with Harvey's conditions for employment – an organization of local women to consult on repairs and redesign of the one-room schoolhouse. Explaining the need for tables and open spaces, Harvey captured the interest of the group to reconsider the school curriculum as well. Before the school year began, Harvey convened a home economics club, beginning discussions about alternatives to traditional methods that no longer fit well with families' daily circumstances. Those lessons served as a model for a school curriculum that would center on methods to increase both home and farm efficiencies. Turner argued that if community women were behind the new curriculum, then the school's influence could be spread because each child would bring home new knowledge and practices to every family.

One immediate problem for the plan was the community's pattern of literacy use.

> The lamps are not lit at night. Writing a letter is a special chore, and is put off as long as possible. Reading and writing are so little a part of the normal routine of life that all facility disappears. They know how to read and write, but it is such hard work that there is no pleasure and very little profit in it.
>
> *(p. 17)*

Without these routines, the community was trapped with only its own ideas. Harvey's remedy was to emphasize the utility and development of literacy at school and through the clubs. At school, each day began by reading of a morning message of community events (similar to the Quincy Method). First-year students would participate in reading the sentences in unison with the older students and then practice the reading chorally during formal small-group lessons. Eventually, individual students would read the sentences and then copy them on slates while saying each word aloud. Older students also participated in the morning exercise and then began work on projects, reading and writing to extend and record their progress. Across a week, the morning messages typically repeated some or many of the ideas and words, building vocabulary, a word bank, and habits of reading and writing ideas. For example, one week's lessons chronicled simple events:

January 20
Children, the box of oranges is here.
Ora brought the box in the wagon.
They are nice, yellow, California oranges.
January 21
Winfield, did you eat your orange?
Laura, was your orange sweet? (Several more named questions followed.)
January 22
The oranges were sent from Los An-gel-les, Cal-i-forn-i-a.
They were shipped on a train.
They came by the Wells Fargo Express.
January 23

They came to Kirkville by the Wells Fargo Express.
The train came over the mountains.
It took a long time for the box of oranges to reach Kirkville.

(pp. 246–247)

Dewey noted that the topics in the morning messages supplied the curriculum across subject areas. Where is California? Which mountains? How do oranges grow? What keeps them fresh? Why are they sweet? What does shipped mean on land? Why not ship by wagon all the way? Each topic led to content discussions and exploration – orally for the young and in print for the older students. And the messages supplied reading material for all in the form of a short weekly newspaper, providing students with reasons to revive, request, and read the local weekly newspaper at home.

In order to supply reading material for community members, Harvey made arrangements with the State Library Commission to have a travelling library reside at the Porter school each year. The women's club arranged the library and opened the school in the evenings in order to permit the working public to visit. Harvey negotiated with the university's agricultural extension to deliver seminars in Porter, using the school for its meetings and leaving literature on farming efficiency on the shelves as a part of the school's permanent collection. The older students used these texts to spread the ideas to farmers too busy to frequent the library or attend the seminars, and they demonstrated the routines of keeping records through their efforts to keep track of the books and other texts. According to Dewey, the clubs, school curriculum, and library attracted families to the renovated school building as the new center of the community, challenging the social isolation of farming and rural households and providing space and information for discussion of new economics of farming and community development. In a relatively short time of five years, Dewey believed that the Porter School and Turner's work demonstrated a model of what schools could do for rural America, providing community members with viable alternatives, using new problem-solving skills to remain on the farm in a more vital community or to follow their interest elsewhere.

Both *Schools of Tomorrow* and *New Schools for Old* ended with chapters describing the theoretical need for and actual connections between schools and democracy. The Deweys considered these schools successful academically and socially because they became vital parts of the communities they served. Students learned to think, to question, to plan and to act, helping them to make sense of themselves and their lives and preparing them for the changes that would come in their lifetimes. Evelyn Dewey wrote, "American education has a big lesson to learn from such schools. What we need is not a certain system, nor a lot of new methods and equipment, but a direction, a conscious purpose towards which the school shall strive ... that of educating for democracy" (Dewey, 1919, p. 331). In order to move in the direction of that ideal, children in school must be allowed freedom so that they will know what its use means when they become the controlling body, and they must be allowed to develop active qualities of initiative, independence, and resourcefulness, before the abuses and failures of democracy will disappear.

(Dewey & Dewey, 1915, p. 304)

Every prospective teacher should learn the meaning and the results for the classroom of two ideas: First, that every school must be adapted to its own particular neighborhood, so that the pupils may gain an understanding of their child-world; and second that what is today the end, reading, writing, all subjects, is merely the means by which she may lead pupils to the understanding of the larger world which they should know as adults.

(Dewey, 1919, p. 324)

To avoid leaving the impression that the Laboratory School, schools of tomorrow and the Porter School were the norm, I offer a quote from a review of John Dewey's *Democracy and Education* (1916).

If we could be sure that the abandonment of the present method of teaching reading and the adoption of various practical forms of activity would result in no poorer reading than we now have, undoubtedly there would be a feeling of great relief on all sides, but the fact is that we do not dare give up our present form of reading until we have something better ... it ought to be possible to demonstrate this with such clearness and definiteness on the basis of scientific studies that we should have more than a mere description of reforms.

(Elementary School Journal, 1916, pp. 273–274)

5

SELF AND SOCIETY

I have used frequently in what precedes the words "progressive" and "new" education. I do not wish to close however without recording my firm belief that the fundamental issues is not of new versus old nor of progressive against traditional education, but a question of what anything whatever must be to be worthy of the name education. I am not, I hope and believe, in favor of any ends or any methods simply because the name progressive may be applied to them.

John Dewey

Between the world wars, progressive educators worked to define the delicate balance between individual and social needs. Dewey argued that the individual could not be realized outside of social commitments and that society could not possibly overcome its class-based repressions without individuals being free and able to develop themselves fully. Although contemporary personal needs and societal roles were not always well aligned, Dewey believed that they could and should be harmonious if both true democracy and freedom were to be realized. Remade schools were the public institution to harness that dialectic by offering children from all walks of life opportunities to make sense of the fragmented realities of capitalism within their personal lives and communities. Within the protected spaces of classrooms, students and teachers would inquire about which practices were worthy of the name "education." Even the most devoted progressive educators found Deweyian inquiries challenging during the social and economic consequences of the Great War, the emergence of modernism in America, the collapse of the world financial system, the rise of social welfare regulations, and political, economic, and social preparations for the Good War.

Child-Centered Pedagogy

> In the first place, experimental education represented a negative response to the deadly, stereotyped, mechanical, and doctrinaire form of education which prevailed everywhere in America. In the second place, experimental education contributed a positive response to liberalism and expression, especially self-expression.... Expressionism was a natural consequence of a culture in which such standards as remained effective were merely those of middle class conventionality or hypocrisy. Experimental education was, then, a revolt against cultural mediocrity. Naturally, its influence was cast on the side of the individual. Like all movements involving the notion of freedom, its purpose was to allow the learner to expand, to discover his latent capacities, to break through the artificial barriers of conformity and formalism, and to reveal fresh, creative possibilities in his relationship to his environment.
>
> *(Linderman, 1929, p. 1)*

Consistent with the Expressionist movement in the arts and newly popular Freudian psychology, child-centered educators sought to create environments to free students' minds, bodies, and spirits from the constraints of traditions and modern puritanism. To reach this goal, teachers worked to dismantle the compartmentalized knowledge of the traditional curriculum, engage students in the creation of knowledge, and infuse their classrooms with ideas, talk, and movement in order to develop, express, and clarify their characters and talents. Oral and written languages were essential tools for this work, but they were not to be privileged over play, emotions, and self-direction within children's school experiences. Child-centered progressives assumed that graduates would take these new habits into the world to disrupt the structures that kept the unjust status quo in place, building new social relationships that encouraged continuous self-development. Adopting this stance for themselves, they engaged frequently in inquiries to identify the best educative practices. This experimental disposition challenged the existing structures of schooling as well as the social forces calling for the scientific management of schools. As Dewey (1928b) explained:

> There is no way to discover what is 'more truly educational' except by the continuation of the educational act itself. The discovery is never made; it is always in the making. It may conduce to immediate use or momentary efficiency to seek an answer for questions outside of education, in some material which already has scientific prestige. But such a seeking is an abdication, a surrender. In the end, it only lessens the chances that education in actual operation will provide the materials for an improved science. It arrests growth; it prevents the thinking that is the final source of all progress.

Play

In 1914, Caroline Pratt, Helen Marot and Edna Smith established The Play School (later The City and Country School) for six children in a three-room apartment in New York City. The school was designed around the seriousness of children's play in their coming to understand themselves in the world. The school's curriculum was based on first-hand experiences (trips to parks, stores, the harbor, and later the countryside), and then imaginative portrayals of those experiences through children's play with blocks and everyday objects once they returned to the classroom. In this way, the curriculum was both impressionist (a few small details represented larger experiences and issues) and expressionist (subjective interpretations, not representations) of the world. Pratt (1948) explained:

> Instead of literature being the spur to children's imaginations, we have found that it is quite the other way around – it is their imaginations which stimulates the creation of literature! A child who has been read a story about a fairy living in a flower is far less likely to turn up with a story of his own than a child who has seen a tugboat on the river. The more closely he has observed the tugboat, the more deeply he has been stirred by it, the more eagerly and vividly he will strive to recreate it in building, in drawing, in words. He will not need to borrow the phrases for his creation from literature. He will find them inside himself; he will search them out and put them together, in his urgent need to express a moving experience, and to relive it in the act of recreating it.
>
> (p. 78)

Before age seven, Pratt and Stratton kept children away from books, stressing the oral language surrounding four-to-six-year-olds' experiences and play (see *Before Books*, Pratt & Stanton, 1926). With the help of philanthropist Lucy Sprague Mitchell and the Bureau of Educational Experiments (founded in 1916; Bank Street College today), the Play School teachers began to transcribe the words and speech patterns of the students in the field and at play. From these transcripts and notes, Mitchell wrote stories and descriptions that she then read and discussed with the students. After careful analyses of the impact of "child-based" stories upon students, she concluded that the familiarity of words, subjects, and rhythms helped children to comprehend better, to follow authors' logic and characters' emotions, to extend the stories in order to create their own texts, and to learn to retell and read stories more effectively. Based on her results, Mitchell published the *Here and Now Storybook* (1921), with 41 stories and jingles for preschool and primary grade children and a short essay to teachers and parents, stating that content and language were equally important in children's books. Reading from such texts became a part of the seven-to-twelve-year-olds daily routine as teacher authored texts, students' compositions, and the formal *Here and Now Primers* (1924) joined traditional children's literature in the school library – "the books in it were there because they had been tried out by the teachers and the children – only after they had been tested in actual use" (Pratt, 1948, 143).

This experimental work influenced reading instruction and children's literature. Pratt's emphasis on play as a mediator for past experiences modified the traditional approach to transcribing children's language about their experience (dating at least to Comenius). Rather than simple narrators of experience, children became interpreters of the world having recreated it through symbolic play. The weight of the language and ideas pushed beyond children's connections of spoken and written words. Mitchell's *Here and Now* stories introduced realistic stories for preschool and primary children as a necessary and worthwhile complement to traditional tales and nursery verse, using children's spontaneous speech as a "way in" for listeners and readers. Margaret Wise Brown, Edith Thacher Hurd, and Ruth Krauss started to write for children while enrolled in Mitchell's the Cooperative School for Student Teachers or the Writer's Laboratory. Others and they began a new genre – realistic fiction for preschool and primary children.

Emotions

> The Bureau of Educational Experiments began a program of measuring the very young in our nursery school at regular intervals. At once, Dr. Lincoln ran into difficulties when she began to measure height – or length – as measurements were taken when the babies were lying down. They wiggled. They seemed to be made of rubber – shorter one day than the day before. In the Child Research Institute at Minneapolis, they put the babies into casts so they couldn't wiggle. They got the measurements. And they weren't interested in the wiggle. We were. Nor were they bothered that casts might be an emotional strain to the babies. Again, we were interested more than in the measurements. Wiggling was an interesting behavior in young children. Emotions were a very important part of children.
>
> *(Mitchell, 1953, p. 460)*

With an interest in tipping the balance even further toward the individual child, Margaret Naumburg opened the Children's School (later Walden) in 1915. She argued, "much of the present social philosophy that wishes to sacrifice the individual to the good of the group is nothing but instinctive herd psychology, translated into modern terms" (1928a, p. 50). She thought that other progressive educators (including Pratt and Dewey by name) neglected the emotional development of children, leaving their personalities and authenticity repressed. Through her own psychoanalysis, Naumburg sought sufficient self-realization to enable her to help children to free themselves from their emotional inhibitions.

> For to us, all prohibitions that lead to nerve strain and repression of normal energy are contrary to the most recent findings of biology, psychology, and education. We have got to discover ways of redirecting and harnessing this vital force of childhood into constructive and creative work.
>
> *(p. 14)*

Through artistic and literary expression and response, each child would discover an authentic self, leading eventually to a better society.

> The early artistic enterprises serve to bring into conscious life the buried material of the child's emotional problems. Gradually, his energies are transformed from unconscious, egocentric attachments, to the wider intercourse of social life. This, indeed, is the function of all art, self expression in forms that are of social and communicable value.
>
> *(Naumburg, 1928a, p. 71)*

Teachers were to provide opportunities for children to represent themselves in multiple contexts without necessarily specifying a course of study. A "[Walden teacher] never suggest a subject, it is always the children's choice. If one says occasionally she doesn't know what to paint, I talk with her until I draw out of her a hidden wish for something she wanted to do but was afraid she couldn't" (Cane, 1926, p. 159). At the Lincoln School (the Columbia University's laboratory school), Hughes Mearns (1925) argued that each child's poetic expressions were, "an outward expression of instinctive insight that must be summoned from the vast deep of our mysterious selves" (p. 28). In a multi-racial elementary school in Los Angeles, Natalie Cole (1940) sought the same "sincerity, directness, and rhythm" in her students' writing that she saw in their painting. She hung children's writing on the classroom walls ("the Wall Newspaper") to afford her fourth-grade students a genuine public. As one wrote:

> I don't like people who is teasing me, and lot of other things, and I don't like the bedbug and don't like to stay home and I don't like people who call me skinnybone and Uncle Sam and dirty pig and a rat, and the worst they call me is a Jap. I am Chinese.
>
> *(p. 130)*

At the Maury School in Richmond, Virginia, teachers organized their reading program around emotional "growth" and personal fulfillment, using five questions to direct their assessment:

1. What evidences are there that children like to read?
2. What evidences are there that they are reading of their own volition?
3. What indications are there that their life is being influenced constructively by ideals and standards derived from reading experience?
4. Are there evidences of growing power of interpretation of life as a result of reading?
5. Are there indications that reading is increasing the capacity for richer living?

(Staff of the Maury School, 1941, p. 38)

Self-Direction

Beyond the primary grades, progressive educators taught reading and writing as part of students' interests, desires, and efforts to make sense of their communities.

In 1918, William Kilpatrick used the *Teachers College Record* to give shape and a name to this practice. When used as "a typical unit of school procedure," he argued, the project method "is the best guarantee of the utilization of the child's natural capacities now too frequently wasted" (p. 334). Students would propose, plan, execute, and evaluate personal and group inquiries, and teachers would guide students to develop skills and strategies necessary to become experts on topics and to express their new knowledge in creative ways. Reading and writing would become habits, "ways of behaving," rather than a known set of skills. "I should hope my boy would consult books where all this accumulated wealth could be found. But I should hope that he would search, and he would find and he would compare, and he would think why, and in the end, he would make his own decision" (Kilpatrick, 1925, p. 213).

Kilpatrick's explanation proved popular as over 60,000 reprints of the journal articles were distributed, and James Hosic (1921) labeled it "a serious and consistent point of view, likely to have far-reaching effects in bringing about the reorganization of the curriculum" (p. 2). Kilpatrick referred all disbelievers concerning the practicality of the "project method" to Elizabeth Colling's (1923) description of a four-year experiment comparing outcomes of the project and traditional curricula in rural Missouri. Students from age six through 16 engaged in four types of projects: excursion, play, hand, and story. Although all types used literacy as a tool, it was featured in the excursion and story projects. Rationales for excursions differed across the three age groupings (6–8, 9–12, and 13–16). The youngest students took trips based on their wonderings about the world. For example, "Carl one day in conference with the other pupils of his group wanted to know why Mrs. Murphy grew sunflowers along the near edge of her vegetable garden" (p. 50). A trip, interviews, and book study ensued, yielding the answer that her garden was designed for maximum yield (stalks shaded the melons from the noon sun). The youngest group produced 58 such reports over the four years of the experiment. The intermediate group engaged in 51 excursion projects – including a repeated outbreak of typhoid at a classmate's home, solving the problem, and holding a community meeting about infectious diseases. The oldest students performed 32 excursions inquiries, including "how Mr. Tut's trial will be conducted in Pineville" (p. 63).

Story projects occupied the first 90 minutes of each school day, allowing students to read, write, listen, tell, and act out stories. Colling reported that the emphasis was always on interpretation and expression with teachers encouraging students to share their responses and to translate stories into other media. For example, Colling reports at length on an intermediate group's exchange about *The Legend of Sleepy Hollow* during a story conference. Students disagree about the plausibility of the plot:

"You know no one would be superstitious enough to believe what Ichabod did."

"There's too much description for me. That's all it is – just describing things."

"I'm sure that it could be true. I'll bet we could make a play out of it, and if things can be acted out, that proves they can happen."

(p. 154)

Colling followed this originating dialogue with 20 pages of negotiation among group members concerning why, how, and when to dramatize the story, a copy of Mary's first draft of a script, peer criticism of that draft, and a playbill for the community performance.

As the result of the experiment, Colling concurred with Kilpatrick and Hosic that the project method was a viable alternative to the Missouri Department of Education's recommended curriculum. On standardized texts for reading comprehension and English composition, the experimental groups outperformed the control groups and national norms at each grade level. Both students and parents found school more engaging in the experimental groups (ranging from 25 percent to 98 percent for students and from 16 to 91 percent for parents over the four years). Attitudes actually declined for students in the traditional groups from 25 to 15 percent across the same period.

Analyses of Child-Centered Schools

Ten years after John and Evelyn Dewey surveyed schools of tomorrow, Harold Rugg and Ann Shumaker (1928) evaluated progressive schools across the Northeast and Midwest against "the six articles of faith" from the Progressive Education Association: freedom, initiative, activity, interest, self-expression, and personality adjustment. After some three hundred pages of examples, they concluded that "the new education has reoriented educational thinking about its true center – the child" (p. 325) and that "not the least of the appeal of the new education is that it offers the same freedom, the same purposeful endeavor, the same encouragement of responsible individuality, the same latitude of initiations and originality to the teacher which it demands for the child" (p. 323). Much more than a hagiography for progressivism, they reported: "in aversion to the doctrine of subject-matter-set-out-to-be-learned, they committed themselves wholeheartedly to the theory of self expression. In doing this, they have tended to minimize the other, equally important, goal of education – tolerant understanding of themselves and of the outstanding characteristics of modern civilization" (pp. viii–ix).

The 33rd Yearbook of the National Society for the Study of Education, *The Activity Movement*, includes testimonials, studies and attacks concerning progressive education in general and child-centered schools specifically. Schools from New York City to Denver to Los Angeles and from Battle Creek to Houston contributed reports promoting activity in the classroom. For example, in Houston,

Oberholtzer (1934) reported significant differences in student activity, creative endeavors, and book reading between experimental and traditional fifth- and sixth-grade classes, resulting in superior scores on the Stanford Achievement Test at year's end as well as increased student and parent satisfaction with schools. Despite such results across the country, advocates of scientific management (e.g. William Bagley, William S. Gray, Ernest Horn, and Arthur Gates) found "activity" at best "a legitimate supplement to a program of systematic and sequential learning" (p. 77), and at worst, "a waste of valuable time" (p. 87). Even scholars sympathetic to progressive education (Boyd Bode, James Hosic, Dewey) worried about the difference between thoughtful and thoughtless activity. In his brief contribution to the Yearbook, Dewey paraphrased his assessment from *The New Republic* series, "The New Education: Ten Years After."

> That the traditional schools have almost wholly evaded consideration of the social potentialities of education is no reason why progressive schools should continue the evasion, even though it be sugared over with esthetic refinements. The time ought to come when no one will be judged to be an educated man or woman who does not have insight into the basic forces of industrial and urban civilization. Only schools which take the lead in bringing about this kind of education can claim to be progressive in any socially significant sense.
>
> *(Dewey, 1930, p. 206)*

In 1932, the Progressive Education Association funded a study to "establish a relationship between schools and college that would permit and encourage reconstruction in the secondary school and find, through exploration and experimentation, how the high school in the United States can serve youth more effectively" (Aiken, 1942, p. 116). Administrators and faculties from 30 urban, suburban, and rural private and public schools volunteered to participate. They agreed to vary their curricula and pedagogy in order

> to develop students who regard education as an enduring quest for meanings rather than credit accumulation; who desire to investigate, to follow the leadings of a subject, to explore new fields of thought – knowing how to budget time, to read well, to use sources of knowledge effectively – and who are experienced in filling obligations which come with membership in the school or community.
>
> *(p. 144)*

In the final reports, study evaluators pointed toward three signature shifts. First, "unified core studies" deployed the content and skills from traditional disciplines within "a cooperative venture in locating, planning, and solving problems" (Giles, McCutchen, & Zechiel, 1942, p. 311). Teachers were challenged to identify moments when strategies, skills and content were immediately relevant and to develop pedagogy that engaged students' acquisition in order to take action. "The greater experience and ability of the teacher will have most influence on the learning of the pupil as it contributes – through questions and classroom arrangements – to stimulation of pupils' thinking" (p. 76).

Second, these challenges became the catalyst for new types of staff development, enabling teachers to be students of their craft in order to design and develop personal, collective and professional resources. "In the course of the Eight Year Study, there has been opportunity to see such faith transform teachers from persons who were merely 'going along' into eager, active individuals who showed unsuspected powers" (p. 16).

Third, the new approaches to learning and teaching required new methods of evaluation. Rather than bring existing tests to bear on the experimental programs, "the plan of evaluation was set up to provide a means by which each school could appraise its work by its purposes" (Tyler, 1936, p. 67). The national evaluation committee asked faculty in each of the 30 schools to name "what [students] should be able to do as a result of these changes?" This process became recursive throughout the study as teachers worked from and on the objectives as a means to modify the ongoing curriculum.

The changes worked. Evaluators compared nearly 1,500 matched pairs of college students who participated in either a traditional or progressive program as they matriculated through one of 300 colleges that had agreed to accept recommended graduates from the 30 schools. Experimental students earned higher grades and more academic honors, were judged to possess more intellectual curiosity and drive, more precise systematic thinking, more resourcefulness, and more concern for contemporary world events, and showed greater participation in the arts and organizations (Chamberlin, Drought, & Scott, 1942). Moreover, in the "study within the study," the 323 students from the six most experimental schools (private: Dalton, Lincoln and Parker; public: Denver, Tulsa, and University School Ohio State) were ranked among the highest students within the original comparisons. Students from experimental schools with large ethnically diverse student bodies were indistinguishable from graduates from traditional small private preparatory high schools.

Social Reconstructionist Pedagogy

There is no good individual apart from some conception of the nature of the good society. Man without human society and human culture is not man. And there is also no good education apart from some conception of the good society. Education is not some pure and mystical essence that remains unchanged from everlasting to everlasting. On the contrary, it is of the earth and must respond to every convulsion or tremor that shakes the planet. It must always be a function of time and circumstance. The great weakness of Progressive Education lies in the fact that it has elaborated no theory of social welfare, unless it be that of anarchy of extreme individualism.

(George Counts, 1932a, p. 258)

Before Counts made this statement to the Progressive Educational Association during the third year of the Great Depression, he had developed a systematic case that even during good times the benefits of public schooling were not distributed equally among social classes. High school drop-out rates demonstrated that few working class students graduated (1922); almost exclusively middle- and upper-class adults served on school boards (1927); new emphases on norms and testing created "scientific" evidence justifying those exclusions (Rugg & Counts, 1927); and business/school alliances provided systematic and intentional pedagogy in order to mold a cheap, orderly, and compliant workforce (1930). In his speech and later pamphlet (1932b), Counts argued:

> If Progressive Education is to be genuinely progressive, it must emancipate itself from the influence of the middle class, face squarely and courageously every social issue, come to grips with life in all of its stark reality, establish an organic relation with the community, develop a realistic and comprehensive theory of welfare, fashion a compelling and challenging vision of human destiny, and become somewhat less frightened than it is today at the bogeys of imposition and indoctrination.
>
> *(1932a, p. 257)*

In order to help progressive educators make these changes, advocates of social reconstruction argued that traditionalist, scientific managers and child-centered progressives promoted capitalist dispositions among students – protestant ethics, competitiveness, and individualism – that would do little to disrupt the unequal status quo. Traditional curriculum featured Western classics already assigned with conformist meanings and values for students to imbibe. Scientific managers divided school content into Carnegie units, measured learning through tests, and ran the school day by the clock, all to train student minds and bodies for industrial work. Although an emphasis on play, emotion, and self-direction were improvements, they argued, child-centered expressionist pedagogy encouraged students to look inward in order to address life's challenges, personalizing social problems and discouraging social movements. Counts and others argued that none of these visions of "reality," "community," or "welfare" would make schools the midwife for true democracy to be born anew during 1930s America. First in a meeting (see *The Educational Frontier*, 1933) and then a journal (*The Social Frontier* 1934–1942), social reconstructionist progressive educators articulated how the midwife could be reformed.

> The [*Social Frontier*] makes no pretense to absolute objectivity and detachment....
> It represents a point of view, it has a frame of reference; it stands on a particular

interpretation of American history ... the *Social Frontier* assumes that the age of individualism in the economy is closing and that an age marked by close integration of social life and collective planning and control is opening. For weal and woe, it accepts as irrevocable this deliverance of the historical process.

(Counts, 1934, pp. 4–5)

Curriculum

The textbook series *Man and His Changing Society* began as an experiment in the fifth- and sixth-grade classrooms at the Lincoln School. Harold Rugg (1941) created 12 pamphlets to help students use economics, geography, history and political science in order to consider the "most insistent problems in life" (p. 274). By reading the texts and completing accompanying activities, students would face America as it is, learning to question the coexistence of poverty with great wealth, racism with the rhetoric of equality and justice, and militarism from a peaceful nation. Later, with a research team, Rugg expanded these lessons into a six-volume middle-school textbook series (Ginn & Co. 1929–1934), designed to help students read the world around them through words, images, statistics, and design. For example, in volume 1, *An Introduction to American Civilization*, Rugg (1929) asked students to consider what makes an American. "First, is it the color of his skin ... the language he speaks ... the clothes he wears ... the job that he holds ... the place where he was born ... his citizenship?" (pp. 66–67).

In *Introduction to Problems in American Culture* (1931), he offered two photographs in juxtaposition:

> This one is of the fine residential neighborhoods in Washington D. C. Notice the wide well kept cement boulevard, the trees, the nice hedges, the large well-built houses, and the automobile.... This is another neighborhood in Washington D. C. Notice the broken pavement in the alley, the lack of trees, the old tenement, and the carts.
>
> *(1931, p. 53)*

In the same volume in reference to a chart on income,

> note the startling differences in income in a year which was regarded as a year of prosperity. In 1929, 36 families in America had more than $5,000,000 to spend; 468 families had more than $1,000,000, 38,146 families had more than $50,000 to spend; and more than 1,000,000 families had less than $1000 on which to live.
>
> *(p. 157)*

In *Changing Governments and Changing Cultures*, Rugg (1932) compared the press coverage of the joint meeting of the National Education Association with the

World Conference on Education and a championship boxing match that were held in New York City at the same time. He explained that eight New York papers devoted 14 times more space to the boxing match. In Chicago, the match received 1,354 column inches and the joint meeting two inches. "Why did these two events receive such different amounts of space.... Two words will state it – Circulation! Advertising! What does it mean to our nation that news comes to us in this way?" (p. 368).

Between 1929 and 1939, these textbooks sold 1.4 million copies. For example, the Little Red Schoolhouse in New York City sought to add social justice to its curriculum during the 1930s. Preschool and primary grade students retained an expressionist child-centered approach. The intermediate students added issues of governance and history to their studies, employing Rugg's textbooks.

> The older groups are ready to face and discuss many of the unsolved problems of the day ... race tolerance, with special reference to the Negro; agricultural problems caused by the new technology, a study made graphic by visits to the forgotten towns and cranberry bogs of New Jersey; submerged labor group; the question of distribution of goods, of wages and hours, of social security.
>
> *(DeLima, 1942, p. 23)*

The textbooks were used "to give the children a realization of the real meaning of democracy and Americanism" (p. 23). During the early 1930s, the New York City Public Education Association began to withdraw its funding from the Little Red Schoolhouse, forcing it to become private.

Although Counts' "Dare Progressive Education Be Progressive" speech had an electric effect on the audience at the 12th Conference of the Progressive Education Association (Redefer, 1948/49), its influence within the association was short-lived. When Counts' Committee on Social and Economic Problems submitted its detailed report a year later, the Progressive Education Association Board rejected it out of hand. Counts published the report privately with a first-page proviso: "The publication of a report of such a Committee does not commit either the Board of Directors or the members of the Association, individually or as a whole, to any program or policy embodied in the Report" (Counts, 1933, p. 1). Ignored in the association, blocked in many public schools as unpatriotic, and eager for action, social reconstructionists developed curriculum and pedagogy in schools for adults around concepts of literacy, equality, collaboration, and agency.

> The whole population need to become students of life and civilization in a new sense and degree and the profession of education must so enlarge its hitherto customary thinking as to accept responsibility for helping as best it can in this new adult field of study.
>
> *(Kilpatrick, 1933, p. 131)*

Literacy

On September 5, 1911 (the night of a full moon), Cora Wilson Stewart and 50 public school teachers began school for Rowan County Kentucky adults "designed primarily to emancipate from illiteracy all those enslaved in its bondage" (Stewart, 1922, p. 9). Intended to educate working adults, schools were only in session when the moon was waxing and then waning from three-quarters to full and back again, allowing workers and spouses to make it safely to schools after work. Stewart's goals were immodest: to eliminate illiteracy within three years; to stimulate communication between locals and those who left recently; to bring progressive ideas to improve work, community, and local culture; and to enable better citizens. "Illiterates are nowhere at a greater disadvantage than at the ballot box, where corrupt men often purchase their birthright for a mess of pottage or cheat them out of it entirely" (p. 182).

Expecting three or four adults at each site, teachers met over 1,200 adults who attended the initial Moonlight School session. To accommodate the numbers, teachers wrote local news on the blackboards until they began to publish a monthly *Rowan County Messenger* that

> enabled the adults to learn to read without the humiliation of reading from a child's primer with its lessons on kittens, dolls and toys; to give them a sense of dignity in being, from the very first lessons, readers of a newspaper; to stimulate their curiosity through news of their neighbors' movements and community occurrences and compel them to complete in quick succession the sentences that followed; to arouse them through the news of educational and civic improvements in other districts to make like progress in their own.
>
> *(pp. 23–24)*

Beyond basic literacy, residents enrolled to study history, civics, health care, home economics, and scientific agriculture. By the fifth year,

> of the 1152 illiterates in the County, only 23 were left, and these were classified. Six were blind or had defective sight; five were invalids languishing on beds of pain; six were imbeciles and epileptics; two had moved in as the session closed; and four could not be induced to learn.
>
> *(p. 56)*

Equality

The Brookwood Labor College opened in 1921 with A. J. Muste as its director. An ordained minister and follower of the Social Gospel, Muste was vice president of the American Federation of Teachers and a former member of the Boston Comradeship that spoke for the immigrant textile workers during their successful wildcat strike in Lawrence in 1919. Enrolment was controlled by a quota system with primarily young unionists of differing religions, unions, geographic regions, and genders attending. All were on scholarships and all – students, faculty, and even visitors – were "pressed into service to cut enough wood for all the fires, peel potatoes and scrub floors between reading assignments" (Hentoff, 1963, p. 59). The curriculum afforded students opportunities to make connections among sophisticated analyses of their local labor relations, the roles of labor in American society, the institutional structures of that society, and the problems of poverty and injustice. Since many Brookwood students stopped formal education at or before grammar school, the texts proved challenging, leading faculty to stress summarizing of complex arguments for newsletters for home unions, writing careful minutes of all meetings, drafting resolutions, revising contract language, and designing effective organizing material.

Graduates with this knowledge and these skills were instrumental in the growth of unions in the late 1920s and later within the Congress of Industrial Workers Organization (CIO). Organizing for the end of child labor, an eight-hour work day for mothers, minimum wages, and public healthcare brought direct reaction from the federal government throughout the 1920s (President Coolidge had been Massachusetts governor during the Lawrence strike, sending the National Guard to quell strikers' activity). Brookwood's militancy brought attacks from the American Federation of Labor, charging faculty with communist sympathies. Despite active defence from John Dewey, "having as its ultimate goal the good life for all men in a social order free from exploitation and based upon control by the workers" (1929a, p. 212), and Sinclair Lewis, "the only self-respecting, keen, and alive educational institution that I have ever known" (as quoted in Levine, 2000, p. 128), Brookwood closed its doors due to financial trouble in 1937.

Collaboration

Like some other contributors to the Educational Frontier, Elsie Clapp (1932) balked at the notion of education as direct analyses of capitalism in order to bring about social reconstruction. In 1934, Clapp had an opportunity to test her hypothesis after being hired as the Director of School and Community Affairs in Arthurdale, West Virginia, a federal homestead community designed to attract families out of the hills after the closing of many coalmines. Although these families had developed habits fit for their lives within the mining communities, Clapp found "they did not expect to be well, did not know how to farm, conduct town meetings, solve civic problems. This adult education was learning to live. The demands of the situation, and their efforts to meet these, taught them. Compare the genuineness and potency of such learning with usual courses in adult education" (1940, p. 123). "On the homestead, teachers took their place as citizens; they and other homesteaders jointly attacked their community problems" (p. 352).

One of the most difficult problems was the change from a company town culture to an economy based on planned production and consumption. Living on credit against subsequent work, as miners' families were forced to do, was no longer possible. Building on the concept of the company store as the community center, Clapp and the Arthurdale teachers organized a store committee in order to design and run a community-owned, cooperatively run general store, which developed community involvement and the idea of living within a budget. By surveying families' needs to determine how to stock the store, community members helped families to plan according to a budget, bargain for better prices from wholesalers, and petition the state and federal government agencies to improve the community's infrastructure for commerce. Once established, the Arthurdale Cooperative Store became a focal point for community education in the new economy, leading to a healthcare program, recreation, night school for adolescents, an agricultural collective, and a school garden to feed the teachers. Once in place, literacy became more than a way to record and distribute information, it became a tool for identifying and addressing community issues.

Agency

> In a real sense, they bring not only their subject with them to Highlander, but they bring their curriculum. That curriculum is their experience. We do what I guess you would think of as peer learning. We think the best teachers of poor people are the poor people themselves. The best teachers about black problems are the black people. The best teachers about Appalachian problems are Appalachians and so on. We're there to help them do what they want and to come to their own conclusions.
>
> *(Myles Horton, April 1975, as quoted in Dropkin & Tobier, 1975, p. 75)*

The educational philosophy of the Highlander Folk School (1932 to present in Tennessee) was (is) straightforward. The solutions to social problems can be found in the collective intelligence and social action of a community once its members believe themselves capable masters of their fate (Adams, 1975). Staff members were to teach by demonstrating their capacities to learn. Classes and workshops were not designed to present information or provide set formulas for problem solving; rather, they were opportunities for participants to name problems, sharpen their questions, find connections between and among issues, make decisions, and then act on their new knowledge and decisions once they returned to their communities. "The greatest education comes from action; the greatest action is the struggle for social justice" (Myles Horton as stated during an interview with Bill Moyer PBS June 1981).

From the 1930s throughout the 1940s, Highlander focused primarily on building a progressive labor movement in the South. The staff worked to support drives toward unionization and to help workers take up positions of leadership in emerging unions, leading to the school becoming the educational center for the

Congress of Industrial Organization in 1940. The first Black speaker at a Highlander labor workshop was in 1934, but because of local community and union leadership opposition, workshops weren't fully integrated until 1942.

In the 1950s and into the 1960s, Highlander faculty changed its focus to civil rights, believing that confronting racism and segregation were the only way to win progressive change within the country. They were instrumental in helping Esau Jenkins, Septima Clark, Dorothy Cotton, and Bernice Robinson organize "citizenship schools," using voting and civil rights as the curriculum to help 100,000 citizens to learn to read, write, and vote. Highlander became a primary meeting place for leaders of the civil rights movement. Rosa Parks, Martin Luther King, Julian Bond, Stokley Carmichael, and many others came to discuss strategies. When Stud Terkel asked Rosa Parks what Highlander had to do with her decision to stay in her bus seat in 1955, she replied, "Everything." The idea for the Students Nonviolent Coordinating Committee (SNCC) was developed at a colleges workshop at Highlander two weeks before the new organization was announced at Shaw University in Raleigh, North Carolina.

Progressive Reading Instruction

Between the world wars, progressive educators remained committed to change society in order to make it freer, more democratic, more just. They acknowledged that the engine for such change would come from the dialectic between self and society. They split, however, on the means to accomplish change. Child-centered advocates worked from the inside out, using play, emotions, and self-direction to cultivate individual expressions of repressed desires for central human values. They stressed developing self-knowledge, self-confidence, and self-expression as the means to a more just democracy. Social reconstructionists acted on what they considered to be collective motives – literacy, equity, collaboration, and agency – in order to remake capitalist society into one that would value people over profits, enabling individuals time and resources to develop themselves continuously.

Child-centered advocates understood literacy as a tool of expression and individuality. By encouraging choice and troubling conventions, reading education would develop each student's interests, talents, and place in the world. By asking students to play with language and structures, teachers would provide spaces and the means for students to define (and redefine) their inner selves while they prepared to engage the world on their own terms. Through close observation and strategic interventions rather than through fidelity to established programs, teachers would help remake the world one reader and writer at a time. Through direct experiences with and artistic representations of reality, confident, creative, and compassionate individuals would not fear freedom or accept the status quo.

Social reconstructionist literacy lessons required unconventional teachers, problem posing curricula, expanded notions of texts, and an activist agenda. Rather than wait for realized children to grow up in order to change the world, literate citizens would engage their peers, posing and addressing problems in their everyday lives. Asking and showing adults what reading was for and what writing could do, teachers prodded their students to identify the social issues behind their apparently personal problems. Developing these feelings of solidarity within – and at times across – groups, teachers and students together exercised the courage to act on their new knowledge and convictions in order to build more inclusive, equitable communities and society. Reading would confront American society with joy and skepticism, and writing would challenge the legitimacy of continuing injustices.

Both groups enjoyed some success and both also met direct resistance. See, for example, O. K. Armstrong's "Treason in Textbooks" (1940) – "The Frontier Thinkers are trying to sell our youth the idea that the American way of life has failed" (p. 8) – and Ann Crockett's "Lollypops vs. Learning" (1940) – "Progressive schools. The only institution this side of heaven that rewards intention as generously as it does accomplishment" (p. 29). In *Educational Wastelands*, Arthur Bestor (1953) charged that progressive educators had "lowered the aims of American public education, setting forth purposes for education so trivial as to forfeit the respect of thoughtful men, and by deliberately divorcing the schools from the disciplines of science and scholarship" (p. 10). In *Quackery in the Public Schools*, Albert Lynd (1953) tracked the problems of progressivism into teachers colleges where teaching candidates were taught to worry about students' emotional development and adjustment and to ignore the liberal arts. In *Why Johnny Can't Read*, Rudolph Flesch (1955) explained that progressives' content and activity interfered with learning to read and write. In 1954, the House Committee on Un-American Activities, the Senate Subcommittee on Internal Security, and the Internal Revenue Service launched full investigations of the Highlander Folk School, hoping to link the labor and civil rights movements with communism. Unable to weather this storm, the Progressive Education Association disbanded and stopped publication of *Progressive Education* in 1957.

6

ALL IN

Our schools are crazy. They do not serve the interests of adults, and they do not serve the interests of young people. They teach "objective" knowledge and its corollary, obedience to authority. They teach avoidance of conflict and obeisance to tradition in the guise of history. They teach equality and democracy while castrating students and controlling teachers. Most of all, they teach people to be silent about what they think and feel, and worst of all, they teach people to pretend that they are saying what they think and feel.

Herbert Kohl

During the first two decades following World War II, as the United States led a successful redevelopment of Western economic and social principles abroad, two social movements challenged a return to a pre-war homeostasis at home. Civil rights advocates demanded universal recognition that Black Americans – whose labor built the economy and whose bodies protected the nation – were citizens and were long overdue equal treatment under the law (14th Amendment, U.S. Constitution, 1868). Despite lawful and violent sanctions, advocates' continued willingness to disrupt the laws and mores of white supremacy led to a series of legal changes: the end of discrimination based on "race, color, religion or national origin" in the American military (Executive Order 9981, 1948), and then throughout society (Civil Rights Act of 1964); a decision that "separate educational facilities are inherently unequal" and school segregation must end (Brown v. Board of Education, Topeka Kansas Decision, 1954); and the abolishment of the first poll tax (24th Amendment, US Constitution, 1964) and then all state and local nuisance barriers to voter registration (Voting Rights Act of 1965).

A second, sometimes overlapping, set of groups pushed for redistribution of economic resources within the emerging richest country in the world. Despite the wartime economic recovery, one quarter of American citizens remained unable to meet their basic human needs of food, shelter, and healthcare. Following John Kenneth Gailbraith's critique of the American production of inequality in *The Affluent Society* (1958), Michael Harrington (1962) brought the invisible *Other America* into view – where 40 million survived on an annual income of less than $3000. In response, President Johnson stated, "This administration today here and now declares an unconditional war on poverty" (1964), leading to the development of an official poverty line by Social Security Administration (set originally at $2995 for an individual), the Food Stamp Act of 1964, the Economic Opportunity Act of 1964 (Job Corp, Work Study, Adult Basic Education, Head Start …), and the Social Security Act of 1965 (Medicare and Medicaid). In 1965, Congress passed the Elementary and Secondary Education Act (ESEA) "in recognition of the special educational needs of low income families."

These and other social movements demanded recognition of difference among Americans and worked to change the institutionalized hierarchies of cultural values that reproduced economic, social, and political inequalities. Changing laws in order to enable recognition and redistribution required sacrifice and struggle to be certain, however, those legal changes were just the beginning of the continuous efforts to overturn the entrenched American definitions of "normal," "mainstream," "common sense," and other similar concepts masking exclusionary cultural values in and out of schools – what Kohl meant by "crazy" and "the guise of history" in the opening quote for this chapter. Although rhetorically intended to benefit all citizens, public schools, Kohl argued, taught children and youth to suppress their deep, primary feelings of worthiness and fairness in order to compete for the illusive American Dream. Positioned by and within this rhetoric of public schooling, students learned to internalize the problems they faced daily as if it were their personal responsibility ("to be silent") and not to imagine the real social issues behind those problems ("to pretend that").

Just as they had not been prepared for social changes at the turn of the 19th century, public schools of the mid-century were unprepared to help children and youth understand these cultural changes. In some ways, schools resisted these progressive changes. In *Growing Up Absurd: Problems of Youth in the Organized Society*, Paul Goodman (1960) argued that America's public schools were a socializing force in service to the bureaucratic, corporate society that prized competition and profits over human development and self-worth. For Goodman, schools produced both the general conformity to the emerging commercialized society and provoked its opposite – the uninterested, maladjusted, and alienated youth – the Beat and the Hood. "Is the harmonious organization to which the young are inadequately socialized, perhaps against human nature, or not worthy of human nature, and *therefore*, there is difficulty in growing up?" (p. 11). Reaching back to Dewey in a sense, Goodman (and the progressive educators who followed) charged that public schooling in its current form was the problem, not the solution, causing alienation because it prepared "kids to take some part in a democratic society that does not need them" (p. 219).

Renewed Critiques of Traditional Schooling

> Even when schools change, they change too slowly. We look at the young and believe we know what they need, and the machinery of education cranks and creaks into gear. But by the time the changes are complete, the young have changed again, and we are ready to handle a generation that has already disappeared. The distance between the world of the young and the schools steadily increases – and so does the damage the schools can do.
>
> *(Marin, Stanley, & Marin, 1975, p. 4)*

Based on their work in schools, a series of teachers began to bring Goodman's critique to bear on students' daily life in and out of schools. John Holt (1964) reported on his students' abilities to perform intellectual tasks in their everyday lives that they failed to take up in his classroom. When asked, one student told Holt, "after all, if you know I can't do anything, then you won't blame me or punish me for not being able to do what I've been told to do." Nat Hentoff (1966) found these capable kids inhabited the inner city as well, arguing that the school, and not the children, was culpable for low achievement at Public School 119 in New York City. With sensational titles – *How Children Fail, Our Children Are Dying, Teaching the Unteachable,* and *The Way It's 'Spozed to Be*, teacher/authors painted pictures of the systemic dulling of students' senses and creativity, supplying example after example of classroom regimes based on intellectual, social, emotional, and physical control through rigid time schedules and textbook curricula.

Beyond critique, these and other progressives suggested and implemented alternatives to the traditions of public schooling. Many found their contemporary model of progressivism in the British infant school movement (Featherstone, 1971). Working from similar philosophical influences – Froebel, Dewey, and Pratt – British teachers featured play, community, and activity in their classrooms, forfeiting desks and lessons in order to open up physical and intellectual spaces. To adopt and adapt this model, American progressive teachers made significant changes in the typical organization and routines of US schools. Whole-class lessons, standardized tests, and published curricula were abandoned for interest centers, individualized pacing of learning, and student choices.

> Open education is a way of thinking about children and learning. It is characterized by openness and trust, by spatial openness of doors and rooms; by openness of time to release and serve children, not to constrain, prescribe, and master them. The curriculum is open to significant choice by adults and children as a function of the needs and interests of each child at each moment. Open education is characterized by an openness of self. Persons are

openly sensitive to and supportive of other persons – not closed off by anxiety, threat, custom and role. Administrators are open to initiatives on the part of teachers; teachers are open to the possibilities inherent in children; children are open to the possibilities inherent in other children, in materials, and in themselves.

(Barth & Rathbone, 1969, p. 74)

At that time, this argument seemed compelling to many with even the New York State Commissioner of Education declaring, "The New York State Education Department, although swamped with work, will give top priority to provision of leadership for school districts throughout the state to do the careful planning necessary to develop sound programs using the open education approach" (Nyquist, 1972, p. 90).

Some of these critics believed schools to be beyond repair, however, and sought to educate children and youth outside the state's educational monopoly. Similar in origins to the Play School, the Little Red Schoolhouse, and the Freedom Schools, these "free schools" were organized around basic progressive principles – intellectual, social, and emotional balance, self-direction, and inquiry – in communities from Watts to the communes of Vermont and from Ann Arbor to Atlanta (Graubard, 1972). Community members – primarily parents – operated these schools according to their definitions of needed social change and free schools therefore differed in structure and process according to racial and socio-economic status within communities.

Each of these types of schools is an alternative, and each is a free school. But one trend emphasizes the role of the school in the community's struggle for freedom, equality and social justice, while the other represents the strongest possible claim for the individual child's freedom in learning and social development.

(Graubard, 1972, p. 7)

For some, even free schools were too restrictive (P. Goodman, 1964; Holt, 1972; Illich, 1970). Their recommendations were to de-school society completely in order to halt the increasing rationalization of individuals' private lives. In place of schools, community life would fulfill the educative responsibilities of societies. The community and all that's in it would become the curriculum, and the ped-agogies would be as diverse as the individuals who lived there. By supplying educational stipends to families, individuals would be free to choose among the alternatives available. Competition to supply valued educational services would regulate the educational market, forcing the ineffective options from the field. In *Compulsory MisEducation*, Paul Goodman (1964) offered this challenge to those who feared this possibility of freedom: "the issue is not whether people are 'good enough' for a particular type of society; rather it is a matter of developing the kind of social institutions that are most conducive to expanding the potentialities we have for intelligence, grace, sociability and freedom" (p. 33).

Reading Instruction in Alternative Settings

> More free schools go to pieces over the question of the 'teaching of hard skills' — and the teaching of reading, in particular — than over any other issue that I know.
>
> *Jonathan Kozol (1972)*

As if beginning anew, these progressive teachers struggled with questions of why, when and how to teach reading and writing — just as their pedagogical ancestors had nearly eighty years before. Although they varied in their levels of commitment, most progressive teachers accepted the rationale that people (regardless of age) learn to read and write for the same reasons they learned to listen and talk as children — to participate as full members in larger social groups with the rewards of pleasure, knowledge, and power. "Printed words are an extension of speech. To read is to move outward toward the world by means of speech. Reading is conversing" (Dennison, 1969, pp. 76–77). Few were in a hurry to push children or students toward letters and print before the children knew what reading was for and what writing could do. Echoing Rousseau, John Holt (1972) explained, "I strongly suspect that we would have many more good readers than we have, and many fewer reading problems, if for all children under the age of ten or even twelve, reading were made illegal" (p. 211). These progressives were willing to wait because they assumed that the job would be made simpler by experience. Paul Goodman (1964) explained.

> A great neurologist tells me that the puzzle is not how to teach reading, but why some children fail to learn to read. Given the amount of exposure that any urban child gets, any normal animal should spontaneously catch on to the code. What prevents? It is almost demonstrable that, for many children, it is precisely going to school that prevents — because of the schools' alien style, banning of spontaneous interest, extrinsic rewards, and punishment. (In many underprivileged schools, the I. Q. steadily falls the longer they go to school.) Many of the backward readers might have had a better chance on the street.
>
> *(p. 26)*

In *The Lives of Children*, George Dennison (1969) provided an eloquent answer to "what to do?" Along with three other adults in four rented rooms within a New York City YMCA, he taught 23 Black, white, and Puerto Rican students from poor families — public school refugees who carried labels of "severe learning and behavior problems." Students were grouped by age: 11 children aged five to eight, seven aged eight to ten, and five aged 11 to 13. Rather than concentrate on instruction as their teachers had in public school, the First Street School teachers "conceived of [them]selves as an environment for growth, and accepted the relationships between the children and ourselves as being the very heart of the school" (p. 4). Dennison shared his relationship/experience with Jose as an example of this point:

> His failure to read should not be described as a problem at all, but a symptom. We need only look at Jose to see what his problems are: shame, fear, resentment, rejection of others and of himself, anxiety, self-contempt, loneliness. None of these were caused by the difficulty of reading printed words – a fact all the more evident if I mention here that Jose, when he came to this country at the age of seven, had been able to read Spanish and had regularly read to his mother (who cannot read) the post cards they received from the literate father who had remained in Puerto Rico. For five years, he had sat in the classrooms of the public school literally growing stupider by the year.
>
> *(p. 79)*

"A reading problem, in short, is not a fact of life, but a fact of school administration. It does not describe Jose, but describes the action performed by the school, i.e., the action of ignoring everything about Jose except his response to printed letters" (p. 77). Dennison sought consul on reading instruction from other free school leaders (Wilbur Pippy from Orson Bean's Fifteenth St. School, Vera B. Williams from the Collaberg School, and Bill Ayers from the Children's Community). Herb Kohl (1973) summarized and added to this advice in *Reading, How To.*

> Reduced to the basics the following are sufficient to enable people to acquire the skill of reading as well as develop the ability to perfect that skill:
>
> 1. a person who knows how to read and is interested in sharing that skill, and who has
> 2. a non-elitist, noncompetitive attitude toward sharing knowledge and information as well as
> 3. some understanding of the process of learning to read and
> 4. a belief that reading is an important human activity that the young should master;
> 5. pencils or pens, writing surfaces and printed material if possible;
> 6. a context for learning in which learners feel secure enough to make mistakes and ask questions;
> 7. respect for the culture and mind of the learner and therefore an ability to understand and use what the student brings to the situation; and finally

8. patience, a sense that there is time to learn.

There are two more conditions that apply specifically to the learner, who should have

9. the ability to use some language as well as reasonably intact senses and
10. a desire to read or at least curiosity about reading. *(pp. xi–xii)*

The Process of Reading/Learning to Read

> A deeper understanding of what is involved in reading, and in learning to read, is far more important for the reading teacher than any expectation of better and more efficacious instructional materials. Nevertheless, I am frequently pressed to elaborate upon what I think are the implications of psycholinguistics for reading instruction, as if psycholinguists have a responsibility to tell teachers what to do. Many teachers have difficulty in accepting that a child might have a better implicit understanding of his intellectual needs than the producers of educational methodology or technology.
>
> *(Smith, 1973, p. vi)*

Beginning in the late 1950s, psycholinguists validated empirically many progressives' understandings of reading and learning to read. Noah Chomsky (1959) challenged behaviorist explanations concerning how language is learned and used. Rather than imitative and mechanical processes, language learning and use were generative, interpretive efforts to produce and comprehend meaning (Miller, 1965). Beneath the surface of an utterance, psycholinguists demonstrated that not all significant features of language have physical representations, that meaning is more than a linear summation of the words uttered, that rules of language use are too complicated and numerous to be taught directly before use, and that humans learn language by using it in purposeful situations. Progressives embraced the notion that children are active and intentional learners, capable of developing facility with language through hypotheses and experience. Moreover, they seized on the need for a rich meaningful environment in which children were free to experiment with language in order to determine which features were salient in expressing their needs and understanding the messages of others. In effect, many progressive classrooms had been psycholinguistic experiments since the turn of the 20th century.

After the 1950s, increased access to public schools meant that teachers encountered a more diverse student population with broader variation within their language use. Sociolinguists sought to explain how social and cultural norms as well as group memberships influence people's use of language (Labov, 1972). Regardless of social class status or race, all students learn to function effectively within specific language environments through hypotheses and experience; however, because social, cultural, economic, and political opportunities and constraints vary across environments, surface level language structures, pronunciations, and vocabularies can differ considerably. In psycholinguistic terms, deep structures map differently onto diverse surface structures within different groups. Sociolinguists argued that institutionalized cultural hierarchies created the difficulties that the poor and minorities experienced with language use and learning at school (Rist, 1970). Rather than valuing the language abilities that students brought with them to school, traditional teachers assumed that different meant deficit and worked vigorously to supplant variations in pronunciation, grammar, and vocabulary with the rules of "standard English."

Progressive reading researchers used these psycholinguistics and sociolinguistics findings in order to challenge the cultural hierarchies in schools. By listening to students read and systematically recording their performance of the printed texts, Kenneth Goodman (1970) found that active readers brought nonvisual information (knowledge of oral language rules, spellings, and the world) to bear on a text right from the start of the reading process, predicting, sampling, and testing what the passage could mean. Rose Marie Weber (1970) explained that "mistakes" in oral representations of the printed page are typically caused by readers' unbalanced processing of the language cues represented in the text and that more proficient readers used more nonvisual information than visual information to make sense efficiently. "Proficient readers make generally successful predictions, but they are also able to recover when they produce miscues which change the meaning in unacceptable ways" (Goodman, 1970, p. 109). From the beginning, these and other researchers (i.e., Carolyn Burke, Yetta Goodman, Dorothy Watson ...) sought to extend teachers' understandings of reading and readers.

With titles such as "Dialect as a Barrier to Reading Comprehension" (1966) and "Let's Dump the Uptight Model of English" (1969), Goodman demonstrated that dialects were not impediments to readers' processing and comprehension of text. He argued that by tracing readers' efforts to make sense of text systematically, teachers could come to understand how all readers use textual cues according to their language, knowledge, and circumstances. With such information, teachers could tailor instruction to fit each child's practices, easing them eventually toward the abilities to switch codes according to their intentions and contexts.

In *Miscue Analysis: Applications to Reading* (Goodman, 1973), teachers shared the impact of psycho- and sociolinguistics on their instruction. Laura Smith employed miscue analysis to make decisions about which texts to include in her classroom, discarding poorly written textbooks for authentic texts that invited and rewarded students' predictions. Katherine Buck found new ways to understand how her "non-native speakers of English" approached classroom texts strategically. Susanne Nieratka used the patterns she found in special education students' reading strategies in order to help them push back into regular classrooms. Vicki Gates described how systematic analysis of students' oral reading led her to reorganize her reading instruction, allowing students choice of text topic, level, and mode of response according to reading strategies and interests:

> The next thing to do, probably the most difficult, is to discard the notion that the teacher has to teach all the time. I turn kids loose with the books,

letting them choose those in which they are interested and they can read. This leaves me free to work with small groups or individual students as their needs arise and/or become apparent....

(Gates, 1973, p. 40)

In a program of 'structured spontaneity' such as this, the needs of the students can be dealt with as they are identified through formal or informal analysis of their miscues.

(p. 43)

During the 1970s, Shirley Brice Heath (1983) worked with teachers in the Piedmont of the Carolinas, helping them to understand and accommodate diverse language practices accompanying students into newly integrated schools. They adopted a sociolinguistic approach to discern how children were socialized into three relatively isolated sub-cultures within a three-mile radius of each other. Separated by race and/or social class, families in these three communities produced distinct ways with words, values, and behavioral patterns in order to continue to function productively. Prior to the study, teachers followed school traditions that valorized only middle-class and white patterns as normal. They had assumed that all differences marked language, cognitive, and behavioral deficits that explained individuals' school failure. With all children being, at least legally, welcomed in public schools, however, Heath and the teachers agreed:

Unless the boundaries between classrooms and communities can be broken, and the flow of cultural patterns between them encouraged, the schools will continue to legitimate and reproduce communities of townspeople who control and limit the potential progress of other communities and who themselves remain untouched by other values and ways of life.

(p. 369)

To cross those boundaries, the teachers began to use the community as the curriculum, paying special attention to how texts (laws, contracts, licensing and employment forms, newspapers, stories ...) influenced and shaped their lives.

Those teachers most concerned about the linkage of their teaching reading and writing to the vocational goals of working-class students decided to ask students to talk about the writing of others which created problems for them and their parents.... [T]he students pointed out that most of the information about social services, warranties, and guarantees, and regulations from the city offices were 'too tough' to read.... [T]he students decided that for the documents to be accessible to their parents, they would have to be rewritten at about fourth or sixth grade level. As the students began to do this rewriting, they were introduced to readability tests and basic word lists....

[T]eachers used student interests in documents from their communities as the stimulus to lead them to numerous other kinds of reading and writing during the term.

(pp. 321–313)

The Process of Writing and Learning to Write

> It is from the children's writing that the teachers have been able to discover what it was that was most important for their pupils to learn at that moment in their classes. Prefabricated curriculum was irrelevant. Teachers had to look to their own knowledge of literature to present images of life that were real and coherent. They found that many of the arbitrary limits placed on children's receptivity and performance disappeared; what was supposedly appropriate at a certain grade level became a mockery of the needs of the children. New criteria and necessities became apparent. It was not grammatical structure, number of words, but human content that determined the lesson.
>
> *(Teachers/Writers Collaborative, Manifesto of the Huntting Conference, 1966)*

The Teachers/Writers Collaborative brought professional writers into public school classrooms in order to join with teachers and students to create a more stimulating and relevant writing curriculum. They found that "all children – white and black, poor and wealthy, city, country and suburban – have an intense inner life that has been revealed in the writings they produced, but which had never been exposed in school" (Wirtschafter, 1968, p. 127). These writings expressed cognitive responses to their experiences and objectified their feelings about who they had become, were becoming and might yet become. In this process, teachers found the beginning of authentic and effective writing pedagogies and sought opportunities for children and adolescents to tell some part of the stories of their lives through different genres.

For these teachers, and the progressive ones who followed, writing instruction emphasized the writing process, student choice of topic and genre, author's voice, revision, and self-expression. Donald Graves (1975) validated these practices systematically by spending a year in first-grade classrooms observing, discussing, and listening to students as they wrote. The opening paragraphs of his subsequent book (1983) tell the story:

> Children want to write. They want to write the first day they attend school. This is no accident. Before they went to school they marked up walls, pavements, newspapers with crayons, chalk pens or pencils ... anything that makes a mark. The child's marks say, "I am."
>
> "No, you aren't," say most school approaches to the teaching of writing. We ignore the child's urge to show what he knows. We underestimate the urge because of a lack of understanding of the writing process and what children do in order to control it. Instead, we take control away from children

and place unnecessary roadblocks in the way of their intentions. Then we say, "They don't want to write. How can I motivate them?"

(p. 3)

When participating in workshop formats, however, Graves found that even the youngest writers demonstrated creativity, risk taking and hypothesis testing that they exhibited in oral language. (Emig, 1971, had already demonstrated this to be true for adolescents.) As teachers moved from the front of the room in order to sit beside writers (Atwell, 1984; Calkins, 1983; Dyson, 1985), they discovered that writing is a social practice during which students talk, draw, read, and write in order to discover and convey the meanings they intend. Like progressive reading researchers, classroom teachers noted that errors offered insight into writer's thinking about meaning and linguistic codes, leading directly to lessons to support writers' development (Hansen, Newkirk, & Graves, 1985). In Graves' words, "receive the student work in such a way that the child is teaching you about what he knows" (1983, p. 78).

> We began our study of what 3, 4, 5, and 6 year old children know about written language with a good deal of optimism, assured that they know much more about print than what teachers and beginning reading and writing programs assume.... What the results of our effort have taught us is that we began not being optimistic enough; that children know much more than we or past researchers have ever dared assume.
>
> *(Harste, Burke, & Woodward, 1981, p. 2)*

By observing and listening to young children's everyday dealings with text (Y. Goodman's *Kidwatching*, see Owocki & Goodman, 2002), Harste, Burke, and Woodward (1984) demonstrated that psychological assumptions of development and the corresponding instructional programs suppressed children's abilities to perform what they know about what reading is for and what writing can do. Moreover, they implied that schooling created the achievement gaps based on "sex, race, and setting" because differences are "not evident in the quality of the responses they make to environmental print" (p. 41). Even the youngest child "informant" displayed organization, intentionality, generativeness, risk-taking, and social action in their efforts to make sense of written language (print, image, design) in specific contexts. With each "discovery" of how language works for and on them, children recalibrate the significance of that new knowledge within their understandings of reading and writing. These researchers and those that followed (Margie Siegel, Kathy Short, Diane Stephens ...) recommended pedagogical and curricular implications that reach back to Dewey's notions of the role of inquiry in learning language, learning with language, and learning about language.

From Goodman to Graves to Harste, Woodward, and Burke, progressive researchers emphasized close attention to children's and students' reading and writing processes in authentic contexts, noting how learning in one form becomes generative and supportive in the other. They demonstrated the importance of a knowledgeable, continuously learning "teacher" who could recognize any student's strengths, and would build upon existing knowledge and use of oral and written language in order to extend students' repertoires in ways that students desired, and that afforded them more choices in their lives. Those researchers and many progressive teachers who followed them began to write about their practices, calling others teachers to engage. Readers, in turn, began to form small study groups of like-minded teachers in order to secure their understandings of this new research and its implications for progressive teaching, and to prepare for "skeptical colleagues, threatened administrators, and bewildered parents" (K. Goodman, 1986, 76).

The Whole Language Umbrella

> Whole language teaching is a grassroots movement among teachers. Deciding to take charge of your own classroom is an act of courage in an era of a shortage of jobs for teachers and a regressive back-to-basics curricular trend. It's particularly scary if you're the only teacher in your school to do so. Many teachers have formed support and study groups.
>
> *(K. Goodman, 1986, p. 76)*

To be certain, these groups radiated from the different hubs of progressive study – the reading process groups from Detroit and Tucson, the writing process from Durham, NH, and New York City, and the inquiry curriculum from Indianapolis and Columbia, SC. However, by the late 1970s, groups populated many states with agendas considering issues from new children's books to running candidates for local school boards. By 1981, representatives from several groups started to meet together during annual conventions of the National Council of Teachers of English (NCTE) and the International Reading Association. At the 1987 NCTE conference, the North American Confederation of Whole Language Teacher Support Groups was formed to explore the possibilities of establishing an international network among interested groups. On February 18, 1989, 3,000 members of that network adopted a constitution to form the Whole Language Umbrella, elected an executive board, and appointed John Dewey and Kenneth Goodman as honorary presidents.

In a supportive critique, Pearson (1989) wrote: "never have I witnessed anything like the rapid spread of the whole-language movement. Pick your metaphor – an epidemic, wildfire, manna from heaven – whole language has spread so rapidly throughout North America that it is a fact of life in literacy curriculum and research" (p. 230). Those metaphoric choices represent challenges that progressive teachers faced. Traditional researchers, teachers, and parents pushed back hard against the whole language "epidemic", fearing the loss of control with each new voice emerging at professional conferences, in classrooms, and from homes. The openness of the philosophy behind the movement and the lack of interest in policing toward a new orthodoxy in order to replace an old one meant the spread of process approaches through whole language often "burned" without restraint. However, the movement was "life sustaining" for those progressive teachers who recognized in it the possibilities of how to create Dewey's notion of an "embryonic community."

Critical Literacy

> How does the 'writing and reading approach' developed by Donald Graves imply a view of curriculum organized around a central pedagogical question: How can we as educators make learning meaningful in order to make it critical and how can we make it critical in order to make it emancipatory? Professor Graves' approach to critical literacy is important in this regard because it contains elements of a language of critique and a language of possibility, both of which are essential to the development of a critical theory of curriculum and pedagogy in which hope becomes practical and despair unconvincing.
>
> (Giroux, 1987, p. 175)

Henry Giroux took the occasion of introducing Donald Graves to connect process approaches of teaching reading and writing explicitly with the progressive project of working for social justice. To do so, he proposed an intermediate step between Graves' notion that writing is a declaration of "I am" and having the freedom to use that declaration in order to participate as a peer with all others in the ongoing negotiations of daily life in a democracy. That step was for teachers and students to become critical, combining Marxist historical materialism, Freudian psychology, and Weber's study of rationalization in order to understand the existing social controls in 20th-century capitalism and racism in order to imagine how a society could be otherwise (Held, 1980). Too often, Giroux implied, progressive teachers neglected the critical in their efforts to empower individuals through reading and writing. That is, they shied away from explicit, in-depth discussions of the underlying economic and cultural ideologies supporting traditional reading and writing instruction, and they stopped at the individual expressive freedom of voice rather than take up the need for collective voices in social actions to unsettle the barriers to participatory parity in and out of schools.

Giroux and others (e.g. Michael Apple, Kris Gutierrez, Bell Hooks, Ira Shor, and Kathleen Weiler) used Paulo Friere's pedagogy to help progressive educators to take the critical step. Friere (1970) argued that schools are partisan sites that "generate and embody support for particular forms of culture as is evident in the school's support for specific ways of speaking, the legitimating of distinct forms of knowledge, the privileging of certain histories and patterns of authority, and the confirmation of particular ways of experiencing and seeing the world" (Giroux, p. 176). These selective traditions validate certain social groups ("Subjects") and relegate others to subordinate status ("Objects"). According to Friere, Objects could become Subjects by developing their understanding of the world and how it works, assuming stances as agents in that work, and acting in the communities to enable participatory parity in social and civic life. Teachers could create spaces that afford all students opportunities to be Subjects through developing critical consciousness – the right to speak, appreciate differences, and develop new knowledge based on their sense of history and place and to act on this critical awareness and knowledge in and out of school.

Rethinking Schools

In 1986, a small group of Milwaukee teachers published a six-page newspaper under the banner, *Rethinking Schools*. In the lead article, kindergarten teacher Rita Tenorio presented a whole language critique of the school districts' reading program, arguing that the prescribed scripted lessons from the mandated Scott Foresman basal silenced both students and teachers. "Students experience reading as a drab prelude to equally drab paper and pencil activities. They come to view books as a source of boredom, rather than as a source of discovery and stimulation" (Tenorio, 1986, p. 1). Moreover, "the systems management approach [of the teachers' manual] is deskilling teachers, robbing them of the opportunity to grapple with the difficult tasks of figuring out what and how to teach" (p. 2). The article and the act of publishing it set a critical agenda for the Rethinking Schools group – "to move things in a progressive way in the Milwaukee Public Schools ... put[ting] forth a clear social justice vision and acting on it" (Peterson, 2011, p. 1). By 1988, the newspaper had 20,000 subscribers including the Milwaukee superintendent of schools, the mayor, and elected school board members.

One of Rethinking Schools' first acts in Milwaukee was to support Riverwest community members who were proposing to fill an empty school building with a "two-way bilingual, whole language, site-based managed neighborhood specialty school" (Bietila & Levine, 1988, p. 1). Riverwest was a racially and linguistically integrated community making strides toward greater civic engagement and development – churches, block clubs, and political groups worked toward local cohesion and a greater voice in the city. Community activists understood the proposed school as an important link between their new program to support preschool-age children and their job programs for adults. They sought a school that would understand each student as a resource for their peers, reinforcing first and second language learning for all. Two of the founding members of the Rethinking Schools group accepted teaching jobs at La Escuela Fratney, writing frequently about the triumphs and the struggles over the first years. Rita Tenorio (1989) reported after the first and second years, commenting on how both languages were validated through the efforts of community trips and family volunteers within the school, but acknowledging the struggles to amass sufficient high-quality children's literature in Spanish with which to carry out necessary immersion in learning to read and write in two languages.

In Portland, OR, William Bigelow (1989), one of the first Rethinking Schools members outside of Milwaukee, demonstrated the language of critique within critical literacy. He asked his students to reconsider Columbus' bloody "discovery" of America on the eve of its 500th anniversary. He began with the official school curriculum – the history textbook – and the processes of critical reading:

> Most of my students have trouble with the idea that a book – especially a textbook – can lie. When I tell them that I want them to argue with, not just read, the printed word, they're not sure what I mean … (p. 635). Textbooks fill students with information masquerading as final truth and then ask students to parrot back the information in end of the chapter 'checkups' … (p. 642). We wanted to assert to students that they shouldn't necessarily trust 'authorities,' but instead need to be active participants in their own learning, peering between lines for unstated assumptions and unasked questions…. As Friere writes, to be an actor for social change one must 'read the word and the world.' We hope that if a student is able to maintain a critical distance from the written work, then it's possible to maintain the same distance from one's society. To stand back, look hard and ask, "Why is it like this? How can I make it better?"
>
> *(p. 643)*

Just before the anniversary, Rethinking Schools published Bigelow's edited book *Rethinking Columbus*, with over 200 pages of texts, poems, and classroom activities to support teachers' and students' critical understanding of that genocide and its implications across time. The volume sold more than 200,000 copies.

In Ridgeway, NJ, after reading an article on Nike Corporation in *Time Magazine for Kids*, Maria Sweeny (1997/98) and her fourth-grade class decided to study the production process of commodities made for children. After a month of watching television shows ("48 Hours" and "Dateline"), reading articles from the internet, the *New York Times*, and corporate and workers' advocacy groups' pamphlets, the class wrote a play about what they had learned. The result, "Justice, Do It", is a nine-scene play about sweatshop and child labor to be performed before the entire school and community (www.rethinkingschools.org/static/publication/rg/rgScript.pdf). Four days before the debut, however, the principal cancelled the performance, arguing that "the play didn't strike a balance" and the play was not "age appropriate" (Nieves, 1997). Despite student and parent protest of censorship, the play was not performed at school that year. However, the Roundabout Theater invited the now fifth-grade students to Broadway in order to present their play on October 27, 1998 (Paller, 1998).

Combining the pre-war call to arms of social reconstructionist with the rediscovery of process approaches of child-centered teachers, critical literacy advocates offered teachers and students a dialectic of critique and hope with which to work toward personal and social transformation. The critique would name institutional and cultural barriers to participatory parity in and out of schools, with particular attention to the maldistribution of social, economic and political resources among groups and the misrecognition of the equal moral worth of all people. The hope would help teachers and students to imagine how redistribution of resources and recognition of difference could make classrooms, schools, and communities into "a larger society which is worthy, lovely, and harmonious" (Dewey, 1907, p. 44). In the acts of synthesis, reading and writing become political weapons and tools with which power circuits could be disrupted and rerouted democratically, signaling the possibility of just politics – that human needs can be addressed within communities.

With the rise of conservative, and then, neoliberal agendas during and after the Reagan Administration, the movements for redistribution and recognition through literacy education fell on hard times (Shannon, 2007). In 1981 with the reauthorization of ESEA, federal officials changed Title 1 to Chapter 1, allowing states the right to use federal funds to improve school-wide reading programs and not solely to support struggling students from poor families. In 1983, the *A Nation at Risk* pitted an emphasis on equity against educational excellence, charging that the liberalization of the curriculum in the 1960s and early 1970s to accommodate new and different students had caused America to lose its international economic standing. Calls for increased national standards measured by standardized tests led to claims that process approaches to teaching reading and writing hindered students' chances to reclaim America's educational and then economic standing. By funding a series of carefully targeted research studies on learning to read, federal officials delegitimized process teaching by brokering a National Reading Panel report (later instantiated in the Reading First Initiative of the reauthorization of the ESEA as the No Child Left Behind law) that featured direct instruction on isolated skills of decoding print using experimentally validated methods only. In this environment, progressive teacher and student voices could only whisper (Goodman, Calfee, & Goodman, 2014).

7

VARIATIONS ON A THEME

First let me say that I believe a critical literacy curriculum needs to be lived and that whatever form it takes should arise from the social and political conditions that unfold in communities in which we live. So I could begin locally and move to more global issues and spaces or it could begin from a global perspective as world events and topics are reflected in the sociopolitical issues that unfold in a community. Given this take on critical literacy, I don't believe it can be traditionally taught. In other words, as teachers, attempting to work through a critical literacy perspective, I believe we need to incorporate a critical stance in our everyday lives in order to find ways to help children understand and analyze the social and political issues around them.

We need to find ways to accept the challenge(s) of the new technological world in which we live to best support children ... who participate in the world with new mindsets, identities, and practices that impact their lives at home, at school, and beyond.

Vivian Vasquez

Leading up to the turn of the 20th century and into the 21st, the flows of capital, information, and bodies across traditional borders seemed to "flatten" the world, enabling more people to participate in the negotiations of an increasingly global society. Facilitated by technological innovations and free trade political agreements, previous historical advantages among nations are being reduced, encouraging commercial and cultural exchanges under new, leveled conditions. Advocates for these changes argue that sustained global economic growth and deeper cultural understandings across differences through communications among people will drive and democratize human progress as never before. As Thomas Friedman declared in *The World is Flat* (2005), globalization will change the 20th-century patterns of everyone's life and accelerate the speed of changes across shorter periods of time and further scales of space.

Vasquez implies that 21st-century teachers face similar challenges to those progressive teachers faced at the turn of the 19th century. Increased capacities for communication and intricate commercial networks disrupt the "established social, political and moral dimensions of everyday lives" (Dewey, 1899), leaving young and old with "habits" that are poorly suited to understand and engage the new potential opportunities (and pitfalls) across larger geographic scales. Now mobility, connectivity, and digitized forms of technology create new ways of social inter- actions both near and far, but they also end personal privacy as we knew it in the 20th century. Although workflow software, outsourcing, offshoring, and supply chain management increase the variety and lower the prices of commodities and services, they also change the conditions of employment, its security, and its availability across rural, suburban and urban areas. At once people are more connected to, but also in constant competition with, people all over the world.

Vasquez accepts Dewey's conception of the roles of schooling in general and literacy instruction in particular. Progressive teachers should help people: under- stand these changes, identify their likely consequences, prepare for the accelerating pace, and negotiate [continuously] new ways to adapt to and to influence these forces. She acknowledges that these roles are not neutral or disinterested. Although teachers should assist students to fit in or cope with the changes, they must also prepare students to participate actively in decisions that enable and direct these changes. That is, schooling and literacy should be directed toward achieving a just democracy by producing social arrangements that will enable everyone to participate as peers in the globalized social life. That means continuing and extending the 20th-century concerns for the economic and cultural dimensions of justice because, clearly, maldistribution of economic resources (surpassing the inequalities of Dewey's time) and misrecognition of cultural standing (under- mining legal gains made in the 1950s and 60s) remain barriers to participatory parity in and out of schools. When discussing this work, Vasquez's conditional language (could, should, attempting) follows Delpit's (1988) and Ellsworth's (1989) advice that progressives become more circumspect and sensitive in their assumptions of similarity and solidarity across human differences and more reflexive about their goals and pedagogies.

For Vasquez, globalization adds a third dimension to teaching for social justice. Progressive curriculum should arise from students' immediate community. However, that point of entry is confounded by the new and rapidly changing relationships between the global and the local. These changes add a political dimension of representation (Fraser, 2009). Vasquez encourages teachers and students to ask: what are the political boundaries in which distribution and recognition claims of injustice can be made and adjudicated? Who is to be included and who is to be excluded when such boundaries are established? By what authority can any body act after jurisdictions are drawn? According to what (whose) rules? What appeared quite clear to most Americans during the American 20th century has become murky during the 21st.

By the language she chooses, Vasquez reaches back across the 130-year history of progressive education in order to articulate her position. As Parker, Pratt, Colling, Clapp, and Dennison practiced, she states that a literacy curriculum "needs to be lived," immediately meaningful in "communities in which we live," and help "children to understand and analyze." Pedagogy is neither fixed ("whatever form it takes") nor finalized ("attempting to work"). Therefore, teachers must learn along with their students because "I don't believe it can be traditionally taught" and sensitive to their interests ("with new mindsets, identities, and practices"). Following Harvey, Rugg, Horton, Clark, and Bigelow, Vasquez advocates for teachers to make the curriculum, tools and pedagogies "accessible to more students" because all are assumed to be interested and interesting in what "arise from" and "unfold in" their daily lives and to possess the capacity to "understand and analyze." Teachers "need to incorporate a critical stance in our everyday lives" in order to demonstrate what reading is for and what writing can do in coming to understand and to act upon the unjust "social and political issues around them."

Other 21st-century progressive teachers reach back in a similar manner as they create curricula and pedagogy with their students. Like the Quincy teachers of the 19th century, they do not follow a singular format for their work because there is no single "progressive method." Rather like their predecessors, the current progressive teachers choose different points of entry according to their beliefs and situations, foregrounding different elements from their progressive values. These differences matter greatly and are worthy subjects for both theoretical and practical discussions within reflexive progressive communities. The similarities are equally important – that is, if progressive teachers seek to contribute to social justice movements in the United States.

Cannot Be Traditionally Taught

In 1993, the Center for Inquiry opened as a school within a school at #92 Elementary in Indianapolis. Forged through negotiations among teachers, parents, faculty from the local campus, and district administrators over a three-year period, the Center's mission was to develop a design for urban schools that supported the basic tenets of the "Quincy Method." All students and teachers have the right to ask and address questions that interest them. With the help of others, they learn all the time and in all environments. Curriculum and learning, then, cannot and does not follow a single or even a typical path for all learners. Therefore, school barriers to these principles should be identified and mitigated, if not overcome. The Center began with 100 students, five teachers and five teaching interns and has spread across multiple public school campuses in Indianapolis and to one in South Carolina. None look alike; all are in continuous processes of development; and each has something to contribute to the struggle for progressive education.

For example, Kate Kuonen's fifth- and sixth-grade students dug deeply into their understandings of video games, exploring the ways that digital games work on and in their lives (Leland, Harste & Kuonen, 2008). Much to the disbelief of her students, Kuonen invited them to bring, play, and discuss games in the classroom, sharing with others their talents, experiences, and advice. Over several months of play, discussion, and note taking, students noticed differences among their perspectives on and commitment to certain types of games, but all agreed that the games were commodities (highly commercially coded to increase sales and not necessarily to inform the public accurately) and that most games were gendered both in content and as social artifacts. Much of the content was directly sexist, and even in their own practices and discussions, female students were often excluded and/or their comments and expertise were discounted. Kuonen's students decided to make their inquiry findings public, designing informational posters and distributing them about the school.

During a second phase of the inquiry, Kuonen learned a pedagogical lesson. According to her original plan, all her students would play a UNICEF "Water Alert" digital game because it broached a subject important to their class theme – "to make the world a better place." However, she found that the game's design undermined her intentions for serious engagement with the topic. Although the game's producers were clearly sincere about the content of the game – the maldistribution of potable water around the world – their design violated basic principles of play, denying multiple points of entry and alternative routes to solutions. Some students declared the game to be "a textbook in disguise" and actively worked to subvert its purpose. In order to "recover" her original intention and recapture interest, Kuonen reopened the inquiry about water security through print and digital sources as well as interviews and observation and then worked toward written and dramatic representations of her students' new expertise for other audiences.

Chris Leland and Jerome Harste (2005) were responsible for the teacher education component of the Center for Inquiry. They intended to prepare progressive urban teachers who would recognize each student's existing cultural capital and academic potential within supportive environments. Those teachers, they believed, would choose to redistribute the benefits of progressive schooling more equitably by teaching in urban schools. Toward that end, Leland and Harste immersed their interns in urban classrooms over two-year periods, encouraging them to engage in discussions with each other and students about issues of justice presented in selected children's literature. In their remarks about this work, Leland and Harste were candid about their struggles to achieve these goals, focusing specifically on interns' resistance to the book discussions and their own inability to help the interns understand how apparently commonsense assumptions and typical everyday practices could possibly contribute to inequalities they observed between their own and their students' lives. In clear language of hope, however, Leland and Harste reported that half of their intern cohorts accepted positions in urban schools because, after they visited schools "at home," they decided that those familiar schools were "too traditional," "based on competition and rewards," and "unfair for any child not right in the middle." Those interns sought and accepted urban jobs "to do what I want to become."

The founding members of the Center for Inquiry in Richland, South Carolina, acknowledged their debt to the Indianapolis group (among others) when they "began dreaming of a better world for public education" (Mills et al., 2014, p. 36). Their dreams echoed those of the progressive teachers that had come before. Compare Evelyn Dewey's sentiments from *New Schools for Old*, "What we need is not a certain system, nor a lot of new methods and equipment, but a direction, a conscious purpose towards which the school shall strive … that of educating for democracy" (Dewey, 1919, p. 331), with the Richland Center for Inquiry mission statement, "When kids pose and investigate issues that matter, they learn so much more than content strategies, they also change their hearts, minds, and actions" (Mills et al., 2014). The inquiries that matter are close at hand and distant as well.

For example, Tim O'Keefe's third-grade students identified an apparent contradiction between the school's efforts to gather food for a local food bank and the waste of considerable amounts of food each day at lunch. Using direct observation and interviews, they identified the centrality of social interaction during the lunch period and a time/taste dynamic in the production of waste. Charting their data concerning students' vegetable preferences, they convinced the cafeteria manager to alter the ordering plan in order to entice students to eat more and waste less. Another example: Scott Johnson invited his fourth- and fifth-grade students to engage in international citizen science by gathering data systematically concerning how seasonal changes affect plants and animals (for the National Phenology Network). Although initially eager, students' interest waned during the daily detailed obligation over long periods. Unwilling to forego the benefits of systematic inquiry or attention to climate (changes), Johnson introduced a variety of national projects for citizen scientists, offering students choices in subject matter and collection procedures. Groups worked diligently and thoughtfully, becoming "experts" on their topics and procedures, but long-term data collection still proved challenging.

What's in a name? The centers for inquiry carry Dewey's notions of knowledge production into the 21st century (Biesta & Burbules, 2003). Students and teachers name problems (as Kuonen and Johnson found, that conjunction "and" is fundamental) with intent to act toward a solution. In order to make that action intelligent, they explore the existing possible alternatives – what others have tried in different contexts and at different times – in order to decide which action might "work" toward achieving their goals in their context. And then they act on their decision, track the consequences, and adjust their actions accordingly. In this way, curriculum and pedagogy are experimental, never finished, and always in development. And the practices of learning and the production of knowledge are not found, but invented, mediated by others, and refined. Center for Inquiry teachers and students named 21st-century problems – commercialism, gendered practices, urban schools, waste, and climate change. They gathered information to develop their expertise, represented their new knowledge for themselves and others, and acted and reacted. Each step challenged barriers to participatory parity. Think about the redistribution of teacher resources to urban schools, the recognition of girls as gamers, and even the representation of the local in climate change. Across the examples, they were becoming better learners, better teachers, better readers, better citizens.

Communities In Which They Live

> Park Forest Elementary is a K-5 school dedicated to the historic purpose of schooling: preparing young people to participate thoughtfully and actively in our democratic society. Our practices are based on the principle that the role of education in a democracy is to sensitize young people to the delicate balance between individual growth and community responsibility.
>
> *(www.scasd.org/parkforest)*

In State College, Pennsylvania, fifty teachers and the principal work daily to foster the social arrangements that permit all students to participate as peers in the social life of the classroom and the school. With a nod to Dewey, they develop apprenticeships in democracy, demonstrating thoughtful and active participation and providing opportunities in which students experience the building of equitable, inclusive communities. Working from the interpersonal practices that students bring with them to school, teachers guide students' participation, orienting them toward inclusive practices, linking their current knowledge with that to be acquired, offering a curriculum with a range of entry points for different students, and keeping the content and literacy challenges within their grasp. Within and across grades, teachers look for changes in students' participation within classroom and school that indicate they are preparing to participate as peers later in the democracy to be built outside of school (Mitra & Serriere, 2015).

In Jennifer Cody's fifth-grade class, she invites students to form groups around research/action projects they would like to engage in, use available print and digital resources in order to develop expertise on the issue, and then, following Muste's encouragement to Brookwood students, act on their new knowledge where and when it might make a difference. The topics for the project are often "problems" that her students recognize in their daily life. For example, one group formed around selections on the lunch menu (Serriere, Mitra, & Cody, 2010). Unable to eat the packaged salads because of religious guidelines or dietary restrictions, six girls sought to expand the menu. Cody encouraged the girls to articulate their concerns based on group memberships and health needs rather than personal preferences. Bolstered by the results of a school-wide survey (90 percent of the student body agreed that more salad options should be available), the girls presented their case of diverse tastes and needs to the school's cafeteria coordinator, who cited U.S. Department of Agriculture requirements, costs, and efficiency as the reasons for the single packaged salad. Discouraged by this bureaucratic response, Cody supported the group's internet searches of school lunch menus from other schools across the country. When they presented their new case to the district-wide cafeteria manager, she proposed a trial run of three packaged options daily. Although not every project had a "positive" outcome, Cody noted new resilience among her students, who – like the gamers in Indianapolis – looked for alternatives when first stymied.

Under the direction of principal Israel Soto, students, teachers, staff, and community members collaborated to transform Public School 57 in East Harlem, New York, into a museum each year (Bryce, 2012). The idea that began in a bilingual after-school arts program for community adults developed over time into Mano a Mano, "an arts-based, interdisciplinary, and thematic approach to curriculum" (p. 179) that positioned all students from kindergarten through eighth grade as museum designers, builders, docents, and performers. Each year, teachers gathered multimodal texts at various levels on the school-wide topic in order to support students' development of content knowledge expertise, and then modeled and mediated students' transmediation of their understandings into print, visual, musical, and performative representations of their new knowledge. Although levels of control over literacy practices differed among students, each produced an individual museum exhibit, collaborated with small groups to produce larger works, and then coordinated with the entire student body in order to prepare the museum for its opening to the community. The openness of the curriculum, the multiple forms of representation, and expectation that all will be successful enabled all participants to engage intellectually, emotionally, socially, and culturally as peers.

Established in 2008, the Evergreen Cooperative Initiative (ECI) seeks to revitalize the Greater University Circle communities in Cleveland, Ohio. Based on the Mondragon Cooperatives Corporation in the Basque region of Spain, ECI is organized around developing green, cooperative businesses (solar energy, greenhouse farming, and laundry), hiring local residents at living wages, and keeping some of the local university's and hospitals' three-billion-dollar budget for goods and services within the community. Within six months of employment every worker is vested as a stock-earning owner of the companies with rights to participate in all company decisions. Along with the redistribution of economic and informational capital through employment, ECI recognizes the cultural and social wealth that exists within these communities already, developing the *Neighborhood Voice*, a citizen journalist communications tool to share ECI news/information, community events, and local stories (Shannon, 2011). Harnessing and developing existing print, photographic, and digital literacies, the *Voice's* few employees invite, scaffold, and celebrate new and old participation from more and more community members. "The Cleveland Model" has been so successful that groups from other cities are considering it as a blueprint for fostering new ways of being and new practices of living that challenge barriers to social justice.

Along with the centers for inquiry, these examples show how sponsored literacy practices shape and are shaped by peoples' acclimation to and participation in specific environments. Park Forest inquiries place reading and writing within a context of civic responsibility. The Public School #57 museums encourage multimodal representations of knowledge. The Evergreen projects juxtapose functional and cultural uses of literacy to further collaboration between businesses and local residents. In order to become members of any of these communities, participants must adopt and adapt those practices, accepting certain values, acquiring specialized knowledge, and learning to use appropriate literacy tools and genres accordingly. In each locale, the leaders seem sensitive to the challenges involved, drawing consciously or unconsciously on sociocultural perspectives to inform their efforts (Hull & Moje, 2010). Their educational goals are linked to topics that matter. Their curricula are open enough to accommodate the variety of interests and levels of literacy that participants bring into the context. They are prepared to mediate students' approximations of sponsored practices through explicit and implicit teaching and performative assessments.

Moreover, the examples include critical twists of those sociocultural principles (Lewis, Enciso, & Moje, 2007). That is, each example afforded participants opportunities to "try on" different identities – advocate, designer, journalist – with support from others. Each addresses issues of power explicitly – negotiating school policy, coordinating the efforts of many groups, and operating as owners. And while the participants are becoming literate members within these communities, they act (are agents) through the practices that they are acquiring. In these ways, the teachers and students work to redistribute resources (at the very least, time and choice), to recognize standing (funds of knowledge, capacity), and to represent the right of each to participate in the decisions that affect their lives (contesting institutional and governmental bureaucracies and global business).

Accessible to More Children

In the North Lawndale neighborhood on the Westside of Chicago, the Legacy Charter School competes with other public grammar schools for students within the open enrollment policies of the Chicago school system. Among its many features, its board explains in its mission statement: "A high quality education must teach the foundations of a just society, ethics, and values that prepare and encourage scholars to participate in the global community with wisdom, understanding, and honesty." The parents and guardians of 500 scholars choose to enroll their children in prekindergarten through eighth grade and to attend the community education programs as well. Founded in 2005 with funding from a city law firm, the Legacy faculty navigates the complex politics of Chicago public schools and city services while helping children and youth make sense of the dimensions of social justice within their community.

First- and second-grade teacher Elizabeth Goss (2009) used the film *A Bug's Tale* and a presidential election to probe her students' interests in and dispositions for taking up the historical and current circumstances of their daily lives. Quoting Dewey on a teacher's role in democracy and Bill Bigelow on social justice teaching, she planned five months of weekly lessons on African American history, working from slavery to the civil rights movement and its impact on the demographics and economic conditions of the Westside. To introduce the topic of slavery, her class watched the animated film that she described as "a Marxist take on the power struggles in the insect world." The six- and seven-year-olds began with issues of *fairness* (ants did all the work; grasshoppers took all the food) and *empathy* (ants' lives were limited; grasshoppers' appeared limitless) and then worked toward issues of *oppression* (the rules favored the grasshoppers; controlled the ants) and *collective action* (so few grasshoppers; so many ants). Goss explained that her students made connections to slavery with references to the film and its themes and to their lives at school and home. When asked to contribute a page to the "If I Were President" class book, students responded, "then I'd ..." stop war, build houses, fund schools, provide healthcare, and make jobs. From the experience, Goss noted changes in the quantity and quality of students' participation in such lessons and of her trust of her students and her willingness to let the students take active roles in determining the curriculum.

The Summer Reading Camp at Penn State University enrolls between thirty and forty elementary and middle-school students, whom school personnel describe as "behind," "struggling," and "learning disabled". Camp serves as a practicum for reading specialist certification candidates, who "try on" a disabilities studies perspective (Simon, 2013), focusing on what the students can do and building on that foundation (Shannon, 2015). On 16 mornings over four weeks, campers and candidates conceive, design, construct, and present a multimodal "museum" based on a single topic (e.g. birds, transportation, weather). Employing Parker's unified curriculum and the performance assessments of the Maury School in Richmond, campers and candidates collaborate concerning the content knowledge necessary for the exhibits; campers apprentice themselves to more literate candidates in developing their content expertise and print representations (reports, poems, songs, stories, diagrams, charts, and jokes); and often, the candidates apprentice themselves to campers as part of the transmediation of that knowledge into paintings, sculptures, mobiles, video games, digital stories, youtubes, and installations. Regardless of their academic labels or individual educational plans, every camper participates in the design of the museum, produces a multimodal exhibit, and stands proudly by his or her exhibit to answer questions during the two hours that the museum is open on the final day of camp. In their case study reports, candidates note the difference in participatory patterns between their observations of campers and the descriptions of their school activities in their permanent records.

At Manzanita SEED, an English/Spanish bilingual immersion school in Oakland California, instruction is split evenly between the two languages across all subjects. Following Kilpatrick's project method and Colling's excursions, the Manzanita teachers use their community as a classroom in order to provide content of the curriculum relevant to students' lives. For example on a topic similar to one Patridge observed in Quincy 130 years earlier, Anne Perrone's third-graders took up the subject of the community's original inhabitants, the Ohlone Tribe. To facilitate conversations and writing in both languages, Perrone and her students visited local historic sites, conducted online research, interviewed experts, and read about the people, flora, and fauna that predated the Catholic/Spanish militarization of the area. Depending on the context, native speakers became the language mentors for their language-learning peers. Once back in their classroom, students expanded their linguistic expressions of their new knowledge by collaborating with others in visual and dramatic expressions (Carter, 2009). Manzanita teachers and parents comment that the authenticity and variety of modes and linguistic frames enable all students to find ways to participate actively in the construction of the curriculum.

It was more than "every child can learn." It was more than building a better school. It was doing school differently. It was thinking outside the box to create a transformative school, not one that would reproduce the inequities of the current system (Manzanita SEED Principal Kathleen Carter as quoted on the National Equity Project website).

By contrasting "better" and "differently," Carter points toward barriers to participatory parity in and out of the classroom. Better implies that the current systems of doing school are appropriate (efficient and effective) and only need greater fidelity from teachers in order to reach the goal that "every child can learn." "Better" has been the goal of scientific management for at least a hundred years. In Carter's words, "better" will only "reproduce the inequities of the current system," dividing students by income, race, language, location and ascribed ableness into those who may participate actively with engaging curricula and those who may not until they have performed acceptably according to official norms. Legacy Charter, Penn State University's Summer Reading Camp, and Manzanita SEED demonstrate by "doing school differently" that those traditional categories of exclusion are actually institutionalized hierarchies of cultural values that deny some students the requisite standing to participate as peers in the construction of the curriculum and life outside schools. In these examples, "doing school differently" approximates at least some of the criteria for culturally relevant pedagogy (Ladson-Billings, 1995). Students experience academic success in projects they find meaningful. Teachers respect difference by building upon and from the funds of knowledge and cultural practices students already possess. Assessments are based on the artifacts students create and the actions they take. Teachers "believed their work was artistry, not a technical task that could be accomplished in a recipe-like fashion" and "exhibited a passion about what they were teaching" (p. 163).

Needs to be Lived ... and Move To (Too!)

According to Dewey, if we seek a socially just democracy, then schools must afford all students the requisite experiences of identifying, insisting on, and enacting democratic justice at some more basic, simplified level. To varying degrees, the centers for inquiry, Park Forest Elementary, Public School 57, Legacy Charter, Summer Reading Camp, and Manzanita SEED are becoming those schools. While not a school, even the Evergreen Cooperative Initiative has limited the scope of their experiment in order to provide protected space for all involved to have "cooperative" experiences. In each example, teachers (broadly defined) made economic, cultural, and social adjustments in order to counter traditional school barriers to participatory parity. Each and all have organized protected spaces where individuals and groups can "try on," "play at," or "take up" the thoughts, values, and actions of just democracy without substantial risks. Because of those moves, the sponsored literacies situated in these spaces look, sound, feel, and perhaps at times even taste and smell different to those in typical school spaces.

Latoya Hardman, an English teacher at Harlem High School, New York, explored different literacies by engaging with them in her classroom (Kinloch, 2010). A transplant from Houston, Texas, Hardman "encouraged students to examine their opinions and experiences through the texts and people I invited into class.... [We learned] more about the local community as we questioned the ways we fit, or did not fit, into it" (p. 84). Together, her students and she faced "the myths" of gentrification (i.e. new, white, and rich are better than old, black or brown, and low income) by first reading stories of Harlem (Sakur, Jordan, Wiesel, and Douglass) and then venturing into the community in order to "respond to the dilemma raised in the book." Once outside the classroom, the words, images, sounds, movements, smells, and tastes of Harlem, accepting, ignoring and resisting the ongoing gentrification, stretched their academic literacies. Their everyday literacies became more legitimate even in their own eyes as they assumed the identities of researchers, teachers, performers, activists, and experts across previously seemingly impenetrable physical, cultural, and emotional boundaries. By making this space together, Hardman recognized that her students "learned more than English. They questioned the changing community as they discovered their roles as informed citizens within it" (p. 86).

After months of preparation, the Occupy Wall Street (OWS) demonstration began on September 17, 2011, with several hundred young citizens protesting the role of wealth in American politics and its apparent cause of growing inequality. In order to evade arrest, protesters retreated to Zuchotti Park, a private space among the buildings. Over the next two months, despite continuous police and government surveillance, several thousand individuals, young and old, joined OWS, erecting tents and creating institutions through collaboration and equal representation. During the first week, someone placed a cardboard box of books on a park bench, and the People's Library was founded as

> a place to engage with what's happening in our country, a means to con-
> tribute their own sentiments through donation of materials, and the literacy
> to see other points of view, perhaps form one of their own, and to express
> criticism in an effective way.
>
> (Norton et al., 2012, p. 9)

The Library Working Group catalogued over 5,000 texts in what they called the LibraryThing, building shelves from plastic tubs, arranging the collection into circulation and reference sections, and covering all resources during rain with clear plastic to assure the police that the sheltered materials were "harmless." Without a circulation desk, the library worked on an honor system and "creative" re-shelving. At 1 a.m. on November 15, police raided the park, clearing it of all Occupiers and confiscating the library's collection. A month later, officials returned 802 usable texts (only two from the reference collection). The Working Group made multiple attempts to re-establish the library in the Park and currently works through mobile units for a storage facility (https://peopleslibrary.wordpress.com). In 2013, a New York City district judge declared that the city government was to pay $366,700 in restitution.

In Room 203 (Columbia, Missouri), Tara Gutshall Rucker has altered the space, time, materials, and practices of her writing instruction (Guthsall & Kuby, 2013; Kuby & Rucker, 2015). To begin, she offered her second-grade students three days to experiment with a wide variety of materials (writing and art supplies) while she observed (watched, listened, and recorded) what they did and made. From these observations, she noted that experimentation with dimension, color, texture, genre, and symbols revealed previously unacknowledged talents among peers and new modes of individual and collaborative engagement. She decided to expand her writing workshop to a studio, sponsoring and accommodating students' explorations in multiple symbol systems and encouraging writers to use the author's chair as a work-in-progress forum for like-minded maker groups. As students became noticed for their expertise, she recognized changes in their patterns of participation and their willingness to consult with others in order to revise their work (improve its effect on audiences). By leveling different modes of writing and providing freedom to choose and act, the students and Rucker created new spaces in which all could "discover" what they meant by their work. By systematically and intentionally following each student's artifact trail across a year, Rucker documented and represented each one becoming a writer.

These examples highlight the reflexive relationships between spaces and types of literacy. The social production of Harlem's past and present, Occupy Wall Street's temporary and lasting presence, and Room 203's writers' studio invited different types of reading and writing, which in turn influenced the ongoing possibilities of those places. In each case, teachers (broadly defined as in OWS) planned their actions but not in the tradition of expecting rationally predictable outcomes. Rather, they planned for porous space and time boundaries, welcoming the literacy practices and texts valued in other spaces and acknowledging that these new engagements could not be easily timetabled. The hybrids of everyday and academic literacies were rich, generative, and resilient, offering protected opportunities for participants to play with ideas, things, and identities while confronting barriers to participatory parity in and out of the institutions. In these spaces and with this time, these teachers built contemporary theories (e.g. Compton-Lilly & Haverson, 2014; Dyson, 2013; Leander & Boldt, 2013) on foundations laid by Dewey, Pratt, Naumburg, and Dennison in the 20th century.

Participate in the World with New Mindsets, Identities, and Practices

Rapid changes in information communication technologies are driving forces in the disruption of 20th-century habits and sensibilities. Although certainly confounded by economic, cultural, and political barriers, many students bring insider mindsets about ICT with them to school – they are prone, if not fully prepared, to work multimodally, use what's at hand, be public with their work, and adapt the messages and media for their purposes. Most of the examples in this chapter show teachers who approach, if not fully adopt, insider mindsets, hoping to mediate students' consumption and production of 21st-century texts. For example, Kate Kuonen from the Center for Inquiry and Elizabeth Goss from Legacy focus on critical consumption of video games and Hollywood films; Tara Gutshall Rucker from Room 203, the teachers at Public School #57 and those in the Penn State Summer Reading Camp provide spaces and support production of multimodal texts; and Jennifer Cody of Park Forest Elementary, Anne Perrone from Manzanita SEED, and Latoya Hardman late of Harlem High combine critical consumption and, at times, critical digital production to counter the texts that construct and maintain barriers to just participation.

At Half Hollow Hills High School, Dix Hills, New York, English teacher Lauren Leigh Kelly offers a Hip Hop Literature and Culture course to acknowledge hip hop's role in popular culture, to give voice to students who are rarely heard, to shift expertise and authority among participants, and to address social issues critically (Kelly, 2016). The course is divided into four themes: hip hop roots, hip hop culture, issues of gender in hip hop, and hip hop's global spread. During the semester, students are to create annotated "mix-tapes" that reflect their interpretation of each theme, present lessons to explore one topic deeply, and compose a hip hop autobiography (from essay, film, music, and graphic representations). Although Kelly assumes a hip hop influence on students' lives, she acknowledges that its influence is mediated by race, gender, and class. To assist students' identifications and analyses of these influences, Kelly teaches the principles of critical media literacy (Kellner & Share, 2007), demonstrating for students how to crack producers' codes and conventions in order to get to the values within any text, to examine the relationships between those values and how power is distributed in and out of the texts, and to react to and act upon those values and relations. Paraphrasing one of her students, Kelly agrees that "you don't have to claim [them]." She concludes that to varying degrees each student meets all four of her course objectives, and she cites Ellsworth when admitting that the critical engagements elicit moments of tension as well as solidarity among students.

> It is important to recognize that the goals of critical hip hop education are not to change students' minds or cause them to disengage with hip hop culture. Rather, the focus is on creating spaces for meaningful dialogue about the media that influence youth identities.
>
> *(Kelly, 2016, p. 536)*

The fifth-grade students of Amelia Szabo and Karen Bierwart teamed with Fertile Ground Director Catherine Sands to use Photovoice methods and software to evaluate the Farm to School (F2S) program in Williamsburg, Massachusetts (Sands et al., 2009). F2S provides reliable markets for local farmers, educates students about the economics of food, and engages students in school gardening programs. At the time of the inquiry, Szabo's and Beirwart's students had participated in the local F2S initiative since its inception when they were kindergarteners. Many had participated in the annual planning of the garden, and all worked weekly to maintain and improve its yield. In order to judge the value of the program, students "snapped" four digital photographs of the program and recorded captions to explain what and why they chose each image to represent their assessment. Along with photos of students working in the garden and its produce, students selected images of the planning documents ("we are involved in every step"); California strawberries ("It was grown on a farm, then driven to a packaging place, then put on a truck, and then driven to a store, then you buy it, *and then* you can eat it"); and the building of a Ramada shade structure ("we chose not to [build a tipi] because it would be stereo-typing the Abenaki"). Throughout the project, Szabo and Bierwart consulted with their students concerning camera techniques, possible criteria for choosing among images, and composing the captions. Different assemblages of students' final products were displayed for 3,000 local residents at school and the public library, the Center for Public Policy and Administration at the University of Massachusetts Amherst, the Boston State House, the Massachusetts, Northeast Regional, and then National Farm to School conferences. After viewing the Photovoice exhibit in Portland, Oregon, the Director of the Michael Field's Agricultural Institute from East Troy, Wisconsin, wrote: "How better to teach students democracy than helping them influence policymakers themselves?" (p. 20).

At Half Hollow Hills High School and Williamsburg Elementary, students use the technologies at hand to explore their local and distant relationships with the world as well as to represent themselves in those relationships (Lankshear & Knobel, 2011). With their teachers' assistance, they identified how the public texts that surround them attempt to teach them what they should know, who they should be, and what they should value. Kelly's students questioned the forms, functions, and content of hip hop texts, researching the "claims" the culture made on their lives. Szabo's and Bierwart's analyzed how ICT texts enable national and global supply chains and what that means for them locally, even personally. Within these practices of critical evaluation (Larson, 2014), students decided whether or not to accept their assigned places within those lessons, and then they appropriated some of the forms and functions of ICT in order to represent their decisions for themselves and others. Szabo and Bierwart mediated students' digital compositions of image, print, and sound, helping them to declare their positions in the world of food consumption and production. After several enabling steps, Kelly consulted with her students as they sifted through their digital artifacts in order to reposition themselves in hip hop culture. In both cases, the projects involved social justice work on economic, cultural, and political dimensions; and the digital technologies afforded students new ways to decode and encode their lives in 21st-century texts.

Doing School Differently

The examples in this chapter demonstrate that progressive teachers practice in all parts of the United States, working with all ages and groups. They follow many of the principles that directed their 20th- and even 19th-century predecessors: they find joy in the work of learning; they seek to understand the world around them and their places within it; they respect the moral worth, cultures and capabilities of their students; and they commit to social justice, dismantling institutional obstacles that prevent some people from full partnership in social and civic life. They work through inquiry – teachers' inquiries about relationships among learning, curriculum, and pedagogy in their classrooms and students' inquiries into the familiar and the exotic (and the exotic in the familiar). Reading and writing in whatever mode are always in service to these inquiries and the discoveries that, as Vasquez said, "arise" and "unfold" from their experiences. During these projects, progressive teachers mediate and students negotiate the dynamics between the person and the group, the personal and the cultural, the individual and the community. These had been the practices in Quincy, MA, Fairhope, AL, Porter, MO, and Los Angeles, CA; at the Lab School, the Moonlight Schools, the Highlander Folk School and the First Street School; and across the South in the Freedom Schools and the country in Eight Year Study schools.

Today's progressive teachers and students do more than repeat the past. They contribute and expand "the well-established principles of teaching" that Francis Parker used to defend and debunk the Quincy Method. As the examples demonstrate, teachers and students experiment with curriculum, tools, and space in order to find the mixes that will invite (and enable) everyone into an activity as peers and then search for relationships, time, and commitments to support changes in each member's participation in the valued practices involved in the activity. Each experiment produces and uses theories and practices of inquiry, sociocultural theories, culturally responsive pedagogies, geographies of learning, and new literacies that feed the continuous experimentation. As Dewey (1928b) argued, "The discovery is never made; it is always in the making" (p. 48), keeping the habits of teaching, learning, and participating from hardening as the world changes. This reflexive character before, during, and after each experiment keeps progressive teachers and students questioning who is included in the invitations, what (who's) values are encoded in the practices, and what should be the scope of those changes in participation. Now, as in the past, the challenges are great; the engagements are deep; and the rewards lead toward justice in the 21st century.

8

CONCLUSION

To Continue

As a verb, struggle means to make a forceful effort to get free of constriction. Since the 19th century, progressives have struggled to overcome institutional barriers and social conventions that justify, reproduce, and hide economic, cultural, and political inequalities. The successes resulting from their efforts to share power with the self-anointed and chosen have been many but also measured. Think graduated income tax within the context of Citizens United, women's suffrage when only 4.2 percent of Fortune 500 companies have female CEOs, or the National Reclamation Act of 1902 in the wake of climate change deniers.

Progressive struggles continue in the hope of realizing a just democracy. For example, the Congressional Progressive Caucus publishes an annual People's Budget, explaining in some detail how federal priorities could put people first. Greenpeace USA witnesses acts against the environment, exposing the consequences of negative industrial externalities. Black Lives Matter intervenes where Black lives are casualties of institutional bias, reinvigorating and extending the civil rights movement. CODEPINK works for peace, advocating a redirection of the U.S. military budget to life-affirming projects. The Next System Project convenes a coalition of progressive individuals and groups to explore different political and economic systems, showing other practical models that yield more just outcomes across these dimensions. In 1937, Dewey framed the importance of such ongoing struggles for teachers.

> In the broad and final sense all institutions are educational in that they operate to form the attitudes, dispositions, abilities, and disabilities that constitute a concrete personality. The principle applies with special force to the school. For it is the main business of the family and the school to influence directly the formation and growth of attitudes and dispositions – emotional, intellectual, and moral. Whether this educative process is carried out in a

predominately democratic or predominantly non-democratic way becomes, therefore, a question of transcendent importance not only for education itself but also for its final effect on all the interests and activities of a society that is committed to a democratic way of life.

(Dewey, 1937, p. 468)

Here, Dewey anticipated the notion of public pedagogy – all institutions present lessons to us concerning what we should know, who we should be, and what we should value. They attempt to recreate us in their own image in order to capture our allegiance to realize their interests. These lessons always involve texts, broadly defined, that are supposed to be read in a particular fashion. Reading education, therefore, is vital in order to crack the codes of these texts, follow their grammars, construct meanings, and decide whether we choose to accept the positions they offer us. Progressives tell us to become careful readers if we value justice for ourselves and others. Moreover, progressive teachers insist that we attend to the processes of reading education if we are to develop the requisite values and dispositions for "a democratic way of life."

What We're Up Against

The progressive struggle in schools continues too. Although they are commenting over a hundred years apart, Quincy's Francis Parker and Manzanita SEED's principal, Kathleen Carter, make the same point:

The methods of the few, in their control of the many, still govern our public schools and to a great degree determine their management.

(Parker, 1884, p. 436)

It was thinking outside the box to create a transformative school, not one that would reproduce the inequities of the current system.

(Carter, 2016, National Equity Project Website)

"The methods of the few" or "the box" are metaphors for social arrangements that seek to instill the cultural values and dispositions that sustain unjust distribution, recognition, and representation among groups, undercutting the possibilities of schooling in a just democracy. Since the NCEE's "A Nation at Risk" report (1983), those arrangements have been designed according to neoliberal values. Neoliberals argue that market competition can solve any economic or social problem. Accordingly, they claim America is falling behind its global competitors because government regulations constrain business market innovations. If deregulated, free markets would engender competition among private and public enterprises, forcing all to allocate resources more effectively and efficiently in order to capture customers (or they will fail). With competitions free from regulation, neoliberals promise economic growth, corporate profits, and trickle-down wealth, enabling more Americans to enjoy the American

Dream. These are the new methods of the few, and they have not worked as argued or as promised.

> America's 20 wealthiest people – a group that could fit comfortably in one single Gulfstream G650 luxury jet – now own more wealth than the bottom half of the American population combined, a total of 152 million people in 57 million households.
>
> *(Collins & Hoxie, 2015, p. 2)*

> Together, African Americans and Hispanics comprised 58% of all prisoners, even though African Americans and Hispanics make up approximately one quarter of the US population. (NAACP, 2016) Think [the] 79 cents [gap for all women] is bad? The pay gap is worse for women of color.
>
> *(AAUW, 2016)*

> An ambitious 12-nation trade accord pushed by President Obama would allow foreign corporations to sue the United States government for actions that undermine their investment 'expectations' and hurt their business.
>
> *(Wiseman, 2015)*

Yet, education policymakers continue the *A Nation at Risk* market-based agenda, refocusing the curriculum away from access and opportunity and toward the skills and knowledge necessary to win those high-paying "Dream" jobs from global competitors. The policymakers argue that unless workers acquire these skills and this knowledge, they have only themselves to blame for personal economic failures. However, the nation needs properly skilled workers for its economy to maintain its global position. Since the 1980s, then, each succeeding reauthorization of ESEA required more rigorous standards from preschool through graduation, tougher texts at each grade, more demanding tests each year, stricter scales to measure success, and more detailed public reporting of outcomes. To make education a market, these policies supported increasing the number of charter schools and vouchers for private tuition. Students have been sorted according to their test scores, and in turn, teachers and schools were sorted by the same measure. These data were aggregated in order to produce algorithms for evidence-based practices of general tendencies of learning and teaching that could redirect "failing" students, teachers, and schools toward effective and efficient use of resources. This is "the box" that constricts students' and teachers' actions in and out of the classroom. In this remarkably candid statement, Bill Gates explains how the box is tied directly to the new methods of the few.

> Identifying common standards is just the starting point. We'll only know if this effort has succeeded, when the curriculum and the tests are aligned to

these standards. Secretary of Education Arne Duncan recently announced that $350 million of the stimulus package will be used to create just these kinds of tests – next generation assessments aligned with the common core. When the tests are aligned with the common standards, the curriculum will line up as well, and it will unleash a powerful market of people providing services for better teaching. For the first time, there will be a large uniform base of customers looking at using products that can help every kid learn and every teacher get better.

(Gates, 2009)

"The box" has not worked either.

Because in every country, students at the bottom of the social class distribution perform worse than students higher in that distribution, U.S. average performance appears to be relatively low partly because we have so many more test takers from the bottom of the social class distribution.

(Carnoy & Rothstein, 2013)

The nation has become a majority of minorities and the common good requires all students to be well educated. Yet, we have embarked on economic and educational paths that systematically privilege only a small percentage of the population. In education, we invest less in children of color and the economically deprived. At the same time, we support a testing regime that measures wealth rather than provides a rich kaleidoscope of experience and knowledge to all.

(Mathis & Trujillo, 2016)

The findings in our study cast serious doubt on the assumption that schools in the private and independent sector – schools that must directly compete for students – produce better outcomes. In fact, the dual remedies of autonomy and competition are fraught with their own difficulties when applied to the real world of education. According to our data, not only might autonomy and competition not work as well as reformers have promised, but they may make matters worse.

(Lubienski & Lubienski, 2016, p. 380)

The four corporations that dominate the U.S. standardized testing market spend millions of dollars lobbying state and federal officials – as well as sometimes hiring them – to persuade them to favor policies that include mandated student assessments, helping to fuel a nearly $2 billion annual testing business, a new analysis shows.

(Strauss, 2015a)

In Reading Education

Despite these results, reading education policymakers turn toward a common core set of standards and testing in order to ensure that all graduates will be career- and college-ready. The National Governors Association contracted the private firm Achieve to produce the template for these common English language arts standards based on its series of surveys of high school graduation requirements, colleges' expectations for first-year students, and business's literacy demands for employees. With generous funding from Battelle, Gates, Cisco, GE, JP Morgan, and Hewitt foundations and Boeing, IBM, Lumina, and State Farm corporations, the final version of the standards was produced in 12 months (2010) under the direction of David Coleman (now president of the College Board). The standards require six major shifts in reading and writing education: increase in the ratio of informational texts to literary texts within assigned reading; use of text to build knowledge; a schedule of text complexity at each grade level; discussions and tests based on the information in the text; writing supported by text-based evidence; and explicit attention to academic vocabulary. Exemplar texts for genre and grade levels were recommended and directions for textbook publishers were made public. The federal government provided financial and regulatory incentives for states to adopt or adapt the common standards, arguing that they would develop critical reading skills and close the income achievement gap.

For at least three reasons, progressive teachers remain skeptical. Many object to the top-down direction of the standards and their corporate origins, commenting on the diminishing role for the public in public education. Since the 1890s, progressives have been consistent in their "concern with humanizing and con-trolling the large aggregates of power built in the preceding decades" (Hofstader, 1965). Here's history teacher Paul Horton from the University of Chicago Laboratory Schools in a letter to the editors of *The Chronicle of Higher Education*:

> In response to several recent columns that embrace the Common Core Standards as a way to prepare students for college, I beg to differ.... What I am attempting to describe is the tip of the corporate iceberg that amounts to corporate control of education policy with very little participation of classroom teachers, parents, or school boards. The idea that the Common Core Standards are the product of a democratic process is a simple misrepresentation of fact – a big lie that GMMB, our education secretary, Bill Gates, Pearson Education, and the Fordham Institute propagate. What many rightfully call corporate education reform has bypassed the democratic process.
>
> *(Horton, 2014)*

A second area of progressive concern is that the standards will develop submissive dispositions among readers. Three of the six shifts for English language arts teach learners to defer to the information in text while reading and writing: knowledge is to be developed through text; answers must be text based; and compositions require textual evidence for legitimacy. Each shift awards increased authority to the ascribed meaning of selected texts, teaching students to read the texts as they are supposed to be read while discounting the experiences, thoughts, beliefs, and desires that they bring to the text. David Coleman, the architect of the standards, bluntly stated the rationale for that authority when speaking to New York State teachers in 2011.

> As you grow up in this world you realize people don't really give a shit about what you feel or think. What they instead care about is can you make an argument with evidence, is there something verifiable behind what you're saying or what you think or feel that you can demonstrate to me.

These shifts offend at least three prominent themes of progressive education. First from Froebel to Pratt to Dennison to Hardman, progressive teachers encouraged learners to develop a reflexive trust of their senses and direct experience over the institutional public pedagogies presented to them as text. In Rousseau's words, "let him know nothing because you have told him, but because he has learnt it for himself" (1762). Second, progressive teachers sought to develop learners' critical doubt about the authority of any text. Remember Wollstonecraft's caution about Rousseau's textual plans for women's education; Rugg's interrogation of photographs and photographers' points of view; Bigelow's encouragement for his students to "peer between the lines for unstated assumptions and unasked questions;" and Vasquez's charge to adopt "a critical stance in our everyday lives." Third, all of progressive education is founded on the affirmation of the emotions of learners and in learning. After all, the first principle of the "Quincy Method" was that learners have a right to be themselves – happy in self-initiated spontaneous activity that makes sense for their level of development without "necessary" outside interventions from others. Put bluntly, progressive teachers do care what learners are thinking and feeling.

Third, progressive teachers take note of the testing regime that accompanies the common English language arts standards, questioning its intentions and its immediate and long-term consequences.

> Although reasonable people have found things of value in the Common Core standards, there is no credible defense to be made for the high stakes uses planned for the new tests. Instead, the Common Core project threatens to reproduce the narrative of public school failure that just led to a decade of bad policy in the name of reform.
>
> *(Karp, 2016, p. 271)*

In a memo released November 14, 2014, Smarter Balanced Assessment Consortium (one of the two federally funded producers of tests for common standards) stated:

The purpose of these [four] descriptors is to specify, in content terms, the knowledge and skills that students display at four levels of achievement (i.e., Level 1, Level 2, Level 3 and Level 4), which in some context may also be described qualitatively in terms such as novice, developing, proficient, advanced ...

(Smarter Balanced, 2014)

Smarter Balanced then listed the estimated percentage of students scoring at each achievement level across grade 3 through 8 and then grade 11:

Level 1 (35 to 28 percent),
Level 2 (27 to 31 percent),
Level 3 (20 to 30 percent), and
Level 4 (18 to 11 percent)

(as shown in Gewertz, 2014)

"In particular, a score of Level 3 and above in 11th grade is meant to suggest conditional evidence of readiness for entry-level, transferable, credit-bearing college courses." What does it mean that the test maker predicts 59 percent of high-school graduates will not test as college-ready after 12 years of schooling? And yet those test scores represent reading skills deemed vital to their economic prosperity.

Proponents of high stakes testing resurrect such determinism presumably without racial overtones, by reducing students, their hopes and dreams for the future to test scores. Effectively, they close the door to the hope of achievement through hard work and academic engagement.

(Williams, 2015)

The first three years of common core testing proved Smarter Balanced estimates to be optimistic. During the first year of implementation of common core testing, the number of passing students dropped by as much as 40 percent in many states, and they haven't recovered much since then (*Education Week*, 2015). Percentages of passing scores for minority and low-income students often fell to single digits, and "failure" reached well up into the middle class, implying not only that the parenting skills and cultural capital of the poor and working class were suspect, as the "old" test asserted, but also that middle-class parents should worry about their contribution to their children's future economic success. When parents reacted to this new application of the label failure to their children and schools, then secretary of education Arne Duncan expressed surprise:

It's fascinating to me that some of the pushback is coming from, sort of, white suburban moms who – all of a sudden – their child isn't as brilliant as they thought they were and their school isn't quite as good as they thought they were and that's pretty scary. You've bet your house and where you live and everything on, 'My child's going to be prepared.' That can be a punch in the gut.

(as quoted in Strauss, 2013)

Reclaiming a progressive tradition, progressive teachers read, name, and resist the current iterations of the methods of the few and the box. The common sense of the neoliberal values that direct these market-based methods and the unjust, undemocratic standards, tests, outcomes, and tactics of the box are encoded in school and reading educational policies and practices in order to justify the large disparities of power, wealth, and status constructed over the last thirty years. Progressive teachers know that Duncan's "punch in the gut" metaphor is offered not as empathy but as a carefully placed reminder that each community, each school, each family, and ultimately each individual is responsible for its failure to properly adapt to new times by reading the texts as intended and accepting test scores as their academic identity. Although the particulars of the current method and box are new, the intention to use education for control is not. Recall that Parker and Kohl made similar statements about their contemporary methods of the few and the box.

The problem for the aristocracy was to give people education and keep them from exercising the divine gift of choice; to make them believe that they were educated and at the same time to prevent free action of mind.

(Parker, 1884, p. 408)

[Our schools] teach "objective" knowledge and its corollary, obedience to authority.... Most of all, they teach people to be silent about what they think and feel, and worst of all, they teach people to pretend that they are saying what they think and feel.

(Kohl, 1969, p. 116)

The Struggle to Continue

After thirty years, these continued poor outcomes have caused doubts among legislators, parents, and authorities, exposing the methods of the few and creating cracks in the box. There have been noticeable successes, but they have been tempered as well. For example, the passage of the Every Student Succeeds Act countered some of the most regressive provisions of No Child Left Behind and repudiated the Common Core Standards, but from a teacher's point of view "it is fundamentally a test-driven, top-down, remediate-and-penalize law" (Mathis & Trujillo, 2016, p. 667) – only under state and not federal authority. Test failure creeping into the middle classes spawned a nationwide "Opt Out" of testing movement, yet 12 civil rights groups signed a document challenging the movement because "abolishing the test or sabotaging the validity of the results only makes it harder to identify and fix the deep-seated problems in our schools" (as quoted in Strauss, 2015b). And the Common Core Standards officials declared that "the best understanding of what works in classrooms comes from the teachers who are in them," but they published and revised publishers' criteria for curriculum at each grade level (Coleman & Pimentel, 2012). These and other actions invite and enable more people to see the new methods of the few in daily practice and to question their logic and outcomes; at the same time they create spaces for progressive teachers and students to continue the struggle to get free of unjust constrictions.

I hope that the previous seven chapters have made it clear that progressive teachers choose justice and democracy, creating spaces in which learners can approximate valued practices at more simplified levels. Within those spaces, they redistribute the resources of time, movement, and tools, allowing learners to access the affordances of rich curriculum. They recognize the equal moral worth of each class member, the different strengths that they bring to the curriculum, and the divergent paths they will take while developing democratic dispositions and habits of participatory parity. Together, progressive teachers and learners move across geographic and political scales in order to familiarize themselves with the challenges of representation in a global society. Their efforts demonstrate that these experiences should start for all before schooling begins and must continue long after it formally ends.

Through these experiences, learners (and teachers) develop intellectually to be sure, but equally important, they develop emotionally, socially, and physically. They try on and construct various identities, including that of citizen. They learn that there are alternatives to the current unjust status quo in and out of schools. Over time, they develop understanding that learning is inquiry, not the consumption of established facts, values, and skills that are later to be sold in order to "make a living." Moreover, they learn that they should be and are capable of participating as peers with all others in identifying problems, conceiving alternative possible solutions, choosing which one(s) to pursue, implementing the choice(s), evaluating the consequences, and making adjustments according to their progressive goals. In those spaces, they imagine and experience a just society.

As many examples in the book show, reading and writing across symbol systems and media are fundamental to these efforts and imaginings. Across time, progressive reading practices have helped people young and old learn about themselves in the world and declare, "I am," "We are," and "We can." Remember Rousseau dated his memory of his conscious self (his "I am" moment) in the emotions of learning to read to his father. By reading the hip hop culture in themselves, Lauren Leigh Kelly's students claimed "I am" here within this culture. Demonstrating her rationality through reading and writing, Mary Wollstonecraft announced for women, "We are" equal to men. Bringing the art, languages, and cultures from their community in Public School #59, teachers and students demonstrate "We are" Mano a Mano – cultural agents worthy of study and institutional representation. Learning to read and write in Citizenship Schools, disenfranchised African Americans insisted, "We can" vote as peers with all others. In Park Forest Elementary and the Center for Inquiry, students developed their expertise through reading and represented their new knowledge through writing, signaling, "We can" participate in establishing school policies.

The lines between and among these moments intersect many of the literacy practices in progressive classrooms over the last 130 years. In many ways large and small, each moment disrupted barriers to participatory parity and affirmed democracy as a way of life. By moving the goal of reading education from the traditions of imparting skills to the challenges of changing each learner's participation in inquires that matter, progressive teachers favor pluralism over norms, collaboration over competition, and inclusion over separation. In those moments and with those movements, we get glimpses of the best of what it means to be human.

If you have already decided that you are a progressive teacher, then I hope that the examples and explanations in this book brought you comfort and, perhaps, inspiration. You are not alone, impractical, or romantic. If we are to build a just democracy in the 21st century, progressive reading education is essential. If you haven't made a decision, then I hope that this book has added many voices to those already in your head, whispering that there are alternatives in and out of school and inviting you to join the struggle to continue the pursuit of a just democracy in America.

REFERENCES

AAUW (American Association of University Women) (2016). The simple truth about the gender pay gap, Spring. Retrieved 11/16. www.aauw.org/research/the-simple-truth-about-the-gender-pay-gap/

Adams, C. (1871). *Chapters on Erie*. Boston: Johnson Publishing.

Adams, C. (1879/1935). The new departure in the common schools of Quincy. *Elementary School Journal*, 35, 495–504.

Adams, F. (1975). *Unearthing the Seeds of Fire*. Winston-Salem, NC: John C. Blair.

Addams, J. (1899). The subtle problems of charity. *Atlantic Monthly*, February. Retrieved 11/16. www.theatlantic.com/magazine/archive/1899/02/the-subtle-problems-of-charity/306217/

Aiken, W. (1942). *The Story of the Eight-year Study*. New York: Harper & Brothers.

Allington, R. (ed.) (2002). *Big Brother and the National Reading Curriculum*. Portsmouth, NH: Heinemann.

Anderson, R. et al. (1985). *Becoming a Nation of Readers*. National Institute of Education, Washington, DC.

Armstrong, O. K. (1940). Treason in the textbooks. *The American Legion Magazine*, 19, 8–9, 51, 70–72.

Astell, M. (1694). *A Serious Proposal to the Ladies for the Advancement of Their True and Greatest Interest*. London: Wilkins. Retrieved 11/16. https://archive.org/details/seriousproposalt00aste

Atwell, N. (1984). Writing and reading literature from the inside out. *Language Arts*, 61, 240–252.

Barth, R. & Rathbone, C. (1969). Informal education: The Open School. *Center Forum*, 16, 70–74.

Barthes, R. (1975). *The Pleasure of the Text*. New York: Hill & Wang.

Bestor, A. (1953). *Educational Wastelands: A Retreat from Learning in Our Public Schools*. Urbana, IL: University of Illinois Press.

Biesta, G. & Burbules, N. (2003). *Pragmatism and Educational Research*. Lanham, MD: Rowman & Littlefield.

Bietila, S. & Levine, D. (1988). Riverfront neighbors win new Fratney school. *Rethinking Schools*, 2, 3.

Bigelow, B. (1989). Discovering Columbus: Rereading the past. *Language Arts*, 66, 635–643.

Bond, G. & Dykstra, R. (1967). The cooperative research program in first grade reading instruction. *Reading Research Quarterly*, 2, 5–142.

Brown, G. (1900). History. *Elementary School Record*, 1, 72–83.

Bryce, N. (2012). Mano a Mano: Arts-based nonfiction literacy and content area learning. *Language Arts*, 89, 179–193.

Burdkick-Will, J. et al. (2011). Converging evidence for neighborhood effects on children's test scores. In G. Duncan & R. Murnane (eds), *Whither Opportunity? Rising Inequality, Schools, and Children's Life Chances*. New York: Russell Sage Foundation.

Burke, E. (1791/1910). *Reflections on the Revolution in France*. New York: Dutton.

Calkins, L. (1983). *Lessons from a Child: On the Teaching and Learning of Writing*. Portsmouth, NH: Heinemann.

Campbell, J. (1965). *Colonel Francis W. Parker: The Children's Crusader*. New York: Teachers College Press.

Cane, F. (1926). Art in the life of a child. *Progressive Education*, 2, 159–161.

Carlisle, J. & Hiebert, E. (2004). Context and contribution of the research at the Center for Improvement in Early Reading Achievement. *Elementary School Journal*, 105, 128–139.

Carnoy, M. & Rothstein, R. (2013). What do international tests really show about US student performance? Economic Policy Institute, Washington, DC.

Carter, K. (2009). Dual language program deepens learning at SEED. *Seednews*, Fall. Retrieved 11/16. www.oaklandschoolsfoundation.org/wp-content/uploads/SEED_News_Fall_2009.pdf

Chall, J. (1967). *Learning to Read: The Great Debate*. New York: McGraw-Hill.

Chamberlin, D., Chamberlin, E., Drought, N. & Scott, W. (1942). *Did They Succeed in College? The Follow-up Study of the Graduates of the Thirty Schools*. New York: Harper & Brothers.

Chomsky, N. (1959). Review of Verbal Learning by B. F. Skinner. *Language*, 35, 26–58.

Clapp, E. (1932). Reaction to Counts. *Progressive Education*, 9, 265–266.

Clapp, E. (1940). *Community Schools in Action*. New York: Viking.

Cole, N. (1940). *The Arts in the Classroom*. New York: John Day.

Coleman, D. (2011). Bringing the common core to life. *Webinar*, April. Retrieved 11/16. www.breitbart.com/big-government/2014/03/24/architect-of-common-core-david-co leman-people-don-t-really-give-a-s-t-about-what-you-feel-or-what-you-think/

Coleman, D. & Pimentel, S. (2012). Revised publishers' criteria for the Common Core State Standards in English language arts, grades 3–12. Retrieved 11/16. www.corestanda rds.org/assets/Publishers_Criteria_for_3-12.pdf

Colling, E. (1923). *Experiment with the Project Curriculum*. New York: Macmillan.

Collins, C. & Hoxie, J. (2015). Billionaire bonanza: The Forbes 400 and the rest of us. Institute for Policy Studies, Washington, DC.

Comenius, J. A. (1657/1886). *The Great Didactic*. Trans. by M. Keating. London: Adams & Black.

Comenius, J. A. (1657/1887). *Orbis pictus*. Trans. by C. Bordeen. Syracuse, NY: Bordeen Publishers.

Committee of Fifteen (1895). Report of the Committee of Fifteen on elementary education with the reports of the subcommittees. Retrieved 11/16. http://archive.org/details/comm ittelemedu00natirich.

Committee of Ten (1893). Report of the Committee of Ten on secondary school studies. Retrieved 11/16. http://books.google.com/books?id+PfcBAAAAYAAJ&pg=PA3&1p g=PA3#v+onepage&q&f=false.

Compton-Lilly, C. & Haverson, E. (eds) (2014). *Time and Space in Literacy Research*. New York: Routledge.

Counts, G. (1922). *The Selective Character of American Secondary Education*. Chicago: University of Chicago Press.

Counts, G. (1927). *The Social Composition of Boards of Education: A Study in the Social Control of Public Education*. Chicago: University of Chicago Press.

Counts, G. (1930). *The American Road to Culture: A Social Interpretation of Education in the United States*. New York: John Day.

Counts, G. (1932a). Dare progressive educators be progressive? *Progressive Education*, 9, 257–263.

Counts, G. (1932b). *Dare the Schools Build a New Social Order?* New York: John Day.

Counts, G. (1933). *A Call to Teachers of the Nation*. New York: John Day.

Counts, G. (1934). Orientation. *Social Frontier*, 1, 4–5.

Cremin, L. (1961). *The Transformation of the Schools*. New York: Vintage.

Crockett, A. (1940). Lollypops vs. learning. *Saturday Evening Post*, 73, 29, 105–106.

Cuban, L. (1984). *How Teachers Taught*. New York: Longman.

Dearborne, N. (1925). *The Oswego Movement in American Education*. New York: Teachers College, Columbia University.

Defoe, D. (1719). *On the Education of Women*. New York: Colliers (1910). Retrieved 11/16. http://legacy.fordham.edu/halsall/mod/1719defoe-women.asp

DeLima, A. (1942). *The Little Red Schoolhouse*. New York: Macmillan.

Delpit, L. (1986). Skill and other dilemmas of a progressive black educator. *Harvard Educational Review*, 58, 280–298; repub. in George, Diana and John Trimbur (eds), *Reading Culture: Contexts for Critical Reading and Writing*. New York: Pearson/Longman, 2007.

Delpit, L. (1988). The silenced dialogue: Power and pedagogy in educating other people's children. *Harvard Educational Review*, 56, 379–385.

Dennison, G. (1969). *The Lives of Children*. New York: Vintage.

Dewey, E. (1919). *New Schools for Old: Reconstruction of a Community*. New York: Dutton.

Dewey, J. (1888). *The Ethics of Democracy*. Ann Arbor, MI: Anderson & Co.

Dewey, J. (1891a) *Psychology*. New York: Harper & Brothers.

Dewey, J. (1891b). *Outlines of a Critical Theory of Ethics*. Ann Arbor, MI: Michigan Register.

Dewey, J. (1895). Results of child-study applied to education. *Transactions of the Illinois Society of Child Study*, 1, 18–19.

Dewey, J. (1897). The university elementary school: Studies and methods. *University Record*, 1, 42–47.

Dewey, J. (1898). Evolution and ethics. *The Monist*, 8, 321–341.

Dewey, J. (1899). *The School and Society: Being Three Lectures*. Chicago: University of Chicago Press.

Dewey, J. (1901). The situation as regards the course of study. *Educational Review*, 22, 26–49.

Dewey, J. (1907). *The School and Society: Being Three Lectures by John Dewey Supplemented by a Statement of the University Elementary School*. Chicago: University of Chicago Press.

Dewey, J. (1910). *The Influence of Darwin on Philosophy and Other Essays in Contemporary Thought*. New York: H. Holt & Co.

Dewey, J. (1916). *Democracy and Education: An Introduction to the Philosophy of Education*. New York: MacMillan.

Dewey, J. (1920). *The Reconstruction of Philosophy.* New York: H. Holt.

Dewey, J. (1922). *Human Nature and Conduct.* New York: H. Holt.

Dewey, J. (1928a). The house divided against itself. *New Republic,* 56, 268–270.

Dewey, J. (1928b). Progressive education and the science of education. *Progressive Education,* 5, 197–204.

Dewey, J. (1929a). Labor politics and labor education. *New Republic,* 57, 211–214.

Dewey, J. (1929b). *The Quest for Certainty.* New York: Minton, Balch & Co.

Dewey, J. (1930). How much freedom in the new schools? *New Republic,* 58, 203–204.

Dewey, J. (1933). Commentary. In W. Kilpatrick (ed.), *The Educational Frontier.* New York: Appleton-Century.

Dewey, J. (1934). *Art as Experience.* New York: Minton, Balch & Co.

Dewey, J. (1936a). *Education and the Social Order.* New York: League for Industrial Democracy.

Dewey, J. (1936b). The theory of the Chicago experiment. In K. Mayew and A. Edwards (eds), *The Dewey School.* New York: Appleton-Century.

Dewey, J. (1937). Democracy and education administration. *School and Society,* 45, 457–467.

Dewey, J. (1938). *Experience and Education.* New York: Kappa Delta Pi.

Dewey, J. (1946). *Problems of Man.* New York: G. P. Putnam.

Dewey, J. & Dewey, E. (1915). *Schools of Tomorrow.* New York: Dutton.

Dewey, J. & Tufts, J. (1908). *Ethics.* New York: H. Holt & Co.

Douglass, F. (1845). *Narrative of the Life of Frederick Douglass, An American Slave.* Boston: The Anti-slavery Office. Retrieved 11/16. www.ibiblio.org/ebooks/Douglass/Narrative/Douglass_Narrative.pdf

Douglass, F. (1857). West India emancipation. Speech delivered in Canandaigua, NY. Retrieved 11/16. www.blackpast.org/1857-frederick-douglass-if-there-no-struggle-there-no-progress.

Douglass, F. (1894a). Self-made men. Speech delivered in Carlisle, PA. Retrieved 11/16. https://books.google.com/books?id=0WfCAgAAQBAJ&pg=PA125&lpg=PA125&dq=Frederick+Douglass+speech+at+Carlisle+PA+1894&source=bl&ots=SA8QBF58KC&sig=3O4johsp2MHL9HxlqfOgehUKBLA&hl=en&sa=X&ei=szuUVLeIItCIsQShmoHQAw&ved=0CDMQ6AEwAw#v=onepage&q=Frederick%20Douglass%20speech%20at%20Carlisle%20PA%201894&f=false

Douglass, F. (1894b). Blessings of liberty and education. Speech delivered in Manassas, VA. Retrieved 11/16. http://teachingamericanhistory.org/library/document/blessings-of-liberty-and-education/

Dropkin, R. & Tobier, A. (eds) (1975). *Roots of Open Education in America: Reminiscences and Reflections.* New York: Workshop Center for Open Education.

Dyson, A. (1985). Emerging alphabetic literacy in school contexts: Toward defining the gap between school curriculum and the child's mind. *Written Communication,* 1, 5–55.

Dyson, A. (2013). *Rewriting the Basics: Literacy Learning in Children's Cultures.* New York: Teachers College Press.

Education Week (2015). Common core's big test: Tracking 2014–2015 results. November 16. Retrieved 11/16. www.edweek.org/ew/section/multimedia/map-common-core-2015-test-results.html#il

Elementary School Journal (1916). Review of John and Evelyn Dewey's *Schools of Tomorrow.* 16, 271–274.

Ellsworth, E. (1989). Why doesn't this feel empowering? Working through the repressive myths of critical pedagogy. *Harvard Educational Review,* 59, 297–324.

Emig, J. (1971). *The Composing Process of Twelfth Graders*. Urbana, IL: National Council of Teachers of English.

Featherstone, J. (1971). *Schools Where Children Learn*. New York: Liveright.

Finkelstein, B. (1989). *Governing the Young: Teachers' Behavior in Popular American Primary Schools in 19th-Century United States*. New York: Falmer.

Flesch, R. (1955). *Why Johnny Can't Read*. New York: Harper & Row.

Fraser, N. (2009). *Scales of Justice: Reimagining Political Space in a Globalizing World*. New York: Columbia.

Freire, P. (1970). *Pedagogy of the Oppressed*. New York: Seabury.

Friedman, T. (2005). *The World is Flat: A Brief History of the 21st Century*. New York: Farrar, Strauss & Giroux.

Froebel, F. (1826). *The Education of Man*. Trans. W. Hailmann. New York: Appleton & Co.

Gage, B. (2016). More 'progressive' than thou. *New York Times*, January 12, Magazine, 17. Retrieved 11/16.www.nytimes.com/2016/01/17/magazine/more-progressive-than-thou.html?_r=0

Gailbraith, J. K. (1958). *The Affluent Society*. New York: Houghton Mifflin Harcourt.

Gamse, B., Bonlay, B., Fountain, A., Unlu, F., Maree, K., McCall, T. & McCormack, R. (2011). Reading first implementation study 2008–2009. US Department of Education, Washington, DC. Retrieved 11/16. www2.ed.gov/about/offices/list/opepd/ppss/reports.html#readng

Gates, Bill (2009). Address to the National Conference of State Legislatures. Retrieved 11/16. www.youtube.com/watch?v=xtTK_6VKpf4

Gates, V. (1973). Organizing a seventh-grade class based on psycholinguistic insights. In K. Goodman (ed.), *Miscue Analysis: Applications to Reading*. Urbana, IL: ERIC Clearinghouse.

Gee, J. (2001). What is literacy? In P. Shannon (ed.), *Becoming Political Too*. Portsmouth, NH: Heinemann.

Gewertz, C. (2014). Cutoff scores set for common-core tests. *Education Week*, November 17. Retrieved 11/16. www.edweek.org/ew/articles/2014/11/17/13sbac.h34.html

Giles, H., McCuthen, S. & Zechiel, A. (1942). *Adventures in American Education*. Vol. 2: *Explaining the Curriculum*. New York: Harper & Brothers.

Giroux, H. (1987). Critical literacy and student experience: Donald Graves' approach to literacy. *Language Arts*, 64, 175–181.

Goodman, K. (1966). Dialect as a barrier to reading comprehension. *Elementary English*, 42, 852–860.

Goodman, K. (1969). Let's dump the uptight model of English. *Elementary School Journal*, 67, 1–13.

Goodman, K. (1970). Psycholinguistic universals in the reading process. *Journal of Typographical Research*, 4, 103–110.

Goodman, K. (ed.) (1973). *Miscue Analysis: Applications to Reading*. Urbana, IL: ERIC Clearinghouse.

Goodman, K. (1986). *What's Whole in Whole Language?* Portsmouth, NH: Heinemann.

Goodman, K., Calfee, R. & Goodman, Y. (2014). *Whose Knowledge Counts in Government Literacy Policies?* New York: Routledge.

Goodman, P. (1960). *Growing up Absurd*. New York: Vintage.

Goodman, P. (1964). *Compulsory Mis-education and the Community of Scholars*. New York: Vintage.

Goss, E. (2009). If I were president: Teaching social justice in a primary classroom. *Voices of Practitioners: Teacher Research in Early Childhood Education, 4,* 1–14.

Graubard, A. (1972). *An Alternative Education: The Free School Movement in the United States.* Stanford, CA: ERIC Clearinghouse.

Graves, D. (1975). An examination of the writing process of seven-year-old children. *Research in the Teaching of English, 9,* 227–241.

Graves, D. (1983). *Writing: Teachers and Children at Work.* Portsmouth, NH: Heinemann.

Gray, W. S. (1937). The nature and organization of basic instruction in reading. In W. S. Gray (ed.), *The Teaching of Reading: A Second Report. 36th Yearbook of the National Society for the Study of Education, Part 1.* Bloomington, IL: Public School.

Greer, J. (2015). Expanding working-class rhetorical traditions: The moonlight schools and alternative solidarities among Appalachian women, 1911–1920. *College English,* 77, 216–236.

Grossen, B. (1997). *30 Years of Research on Reading.* Santa Cruz, CA: Center for the Future of Teaching and Learning.

Gutshall, T. & Kuby, C. (2013). Students as integral contributors to teacher research. *Talking Points,* 25, 2–8.

Hansen, J., Newkirk, T. & Graves, D. (eds) (1985). *Breaking Ground: Teachers Relate Reading and Writing in Elementary School.* Portsmouth, NH: Heinemann.

Harrington, M. (1962). *The Other America: Poverty in the United States.* New York: Macmillan.

Harste, J., Burke, C. & Woodward, V. (1981). Children, their language, and world: Initial encounters with print. NIE Final Report. Indiana University, Bloomington, IN.

Harste, J., Woodward, V. & Burke, C. (1984). *Language Stories and Literacy Lessons.* Portsmouth, NH: Heinemann.

Heath, S. B. (1983). *Ways with Words: Language, Life and Work in Communities and Classrooms.* Cambridge, UK: Cambridge University Press.

Held, D. (1980). *Introduction to Critical Theory: Horkheimer to Habermas.* Berkeley, CA: University of California.

Hentoff, N. (1963). *Peace Agitator: The Story of A. J. Muste.* New York: Macmillan.

Hentoff, N. (1966). *Our Children Are Dying.* New York: Viking.

Hofstadter, R. (1965). *Anti-intellectualism in American Life.* New York: Knopf.

Holbrook, A. (1872). *Reminiscences of the Happy Life of a Teacher.* Cincinnati, OH: Elm St. Publishing.

Holt, J. (1964). *How Children Fail.* New York: Pitman.

Holt, J. (1972). *Freedom and Beyond.* New York: Dutton.

Horton, P. (2014). Common core standards are the tip of a corporate iceberg. *Chronicle of Higher Education,* June 30. Retrieved 11/16. www.chronicle.com/blogs/letters/comm on-core-standards-are-the-tip-of-a-corporate-iceberg/

Hosic, J. (1921). Editorially speaking. *Journal of Educational Methods,* 1, 1–2.

Huey, E. B. (1908/1968). *The Psychology and Pedagogy of Reading.* Cambridge, MA: MIT.

Hull, G. & Moje, E. (2010). What is the development of literacy the development of? The Understanding Language Initiative Stanford University. Retrieved 11/16. http://ell.sta nford.edu/sites/default/files/pdf/academic-papers/05-Hull%20%26%20Moje%20CC% 20Paper%20FINAL.pdf.

Hunt, L. (2014). *Writing History in the Global Era.* New York: W. W. Norton.

Hutchins, H. (1936). *A Victorian in the Modern World.* New York: Appleton and Co.

Illich, I. (1970). *Deschooling Society.* New York: Harper & Row.

Johnson, L. B. (1964). State of the union address to the U.S. Congress. January 8. Retrieved 12/16. http://civicreflection.org/resources/library/browse/state-of-the-union-address-1964

Johnson, M. (1929). *Youth in the World of Men.* New York: John Daly.

Johnson, M. (1938). *Thirty Years with an Idea.* University, AL: University of Alabama.

Karp, S. (2016). The problems with the common core. In W. Mathis & T. Trujillo (eds.) *Learning for the Federal Market-Based Reforms.* Charlotte, NC: Information Age Publishing.

Kellner, D. & Share, J. (2005). Toward critical media literacy: Core concepts, debates, organization, and policy. *Discourse Studies in the Cultural Politics of Education,* 26, 369–386.

Kelly, L. (2016). You don't have to claim her: Reconstructing black femininity through critical hip hop literacy. *Journal of Adolescent and Adult Literacy,* 59, 529–538.

Kilpatrick, W. (1918). The project method. *Teachers College Record,* 19, 319–335.

Kilpatrick, W. (1925). *Foundations of Methods: Informal Talks with Teachers.* New York: Macmillan.

Kilpatrick, W. (1934). Launching the *Social Frontier. Social Frontier,* 1, 2.

Kilpatrick, W., Bode, B., Dewey, J., Child, J., Raup, B., Hullfish, H. & Thayer, V. (eds) (1933). *The Educational Frontier.* New York: Appleton-Century.

Kinloch, V. (2010). *Harlem on Our Minds: Place, Race and the Literacies of Urban Youth.* New York: Teachers College Press.

Kliebard, H. (1986). *The Struggle of the American Curriculum 1893–1958.* Boston, MA: Routledge & Kegan Paul.

Kohl, H. (1969). *The Open Classroom: A Practical Guide to a New Way of Teaching.* New York: New York Review Book.

Kohl, H. (1973). *Reading, How To.* New York: Bantam.

Kozol, J. (1972). *Free Schools.* Boston: Houghton-Miflin.

Kuby, C. & Rucker, T. (2015). Everyone has a Neil: Possibilities of literacy desiring in writers' studio. *Language Arts,* 92, 314–327.

Labov, W. (1972). *Language in the Inner City: Studies in the Black English Vernacular.* Philadelphia: University of Pennsylvania Press.

Ladson-Billings, G. (1995). But that's just good teaching! The case for culturally relevant pedagogy. *Theory Into Practice,* 34, 159–165.

Lagemann, E. C. (2000). *An Elusive Science: The Troubling History of Educational Research.* Chicago: University of Chicago Press.

Lankshear, C. & Knobel, M. (2011). *New Literacies: Everyday Practices and Social Learning.* 3rd ed. New York: Open University Press.

Larson, J. (2014). *Radical Equality in Education: Starting Over in U.S. Schooling.* New York: Routledge.

Laurie, S. (1884). *John Amos Comenius.* Cambridge, UK. Cambridge University Press.

Leander, K. & Boldt, G. (2013). Rereading "a pedagogy of multiliteracies": Bodies, texts and emergence. *Journal of Literacy Research,* 45, 22–46.

Leland, C. & Harste, J. (2005). Doing what we want to become: Preparing new urban teachers. *Urban Education,* 40, 60–77.

Leland, C., Harste, J. & Kuonen, K. (2009). Unpacking videogames: Understanding and supporting a new ethos. In Y. Kim et al. (eds), *57th Yearbook of the National Reading Conference.* Oak Creek, WI: National Reading Conference.

Levine, A. (2000). Brookwood remembered. In D. DeZure (ed.), *Learning for Change: Landmarks in Teaching and Learning in Higher Education from 'Change' Magazine, 1969–1999.* Sterling, VA: Stylus.

Lewis, C., Enciso, P. & Moje, E. (2007). *Reframing Sociocultural Research on Literacy: Identity, Agency, and Power*. Mahwah, NJ: Lawrence Erlbaum.

Linderman, E. (1929). The origin of experimental education. In M. Schauffer (ed.), *Schools Grow*. New York: Bureau of Educational Experiments.

Lubienski, C. & Lubienski, S. (2016). Reconsidering choice, competition, and autonomy as the remedy in American education. In W. Mathis & T. Trujillo (eds). *Learning from the Federal Market-Based Reforms*. Charlotte, NC: Information Age Publishing.

Lynd, A. (1953). *Quackery in the Public Schools*. New York: Little Brown.

Macaulay, C. (1790). Letters on education. Vol. 3 of J. Todd (ed.), *Female Education in the Age of Enlightenment*. London: Pickering & Chatto (1996).

Maclure, W. (1820). Letter to Marie Fretageot. In A. Bester (ed.), *Education and Reform at New Harmony: Correspondence of William Maclure and Marie Fretageot*. Indianapolis, IN: Indiana Historical Society (1948).

Maclure, W. (1831). *Opinions on Various Subjects*. New Harmony, IN: New Harmony Press.

Macrae, D. (1875). *The American at Home*. Glasgow: Johns Maor.

Makin, B. (1673). *An Essay to Revive the Ancient Education of Gentle Women*. Parkhurst, London. Retrieved 11/16http://digital.library.upenn.edu/women/makin/education/education.html

Marin, P., Stanley, V. & Marin, K. (1975). *The Limits of Schooling*. Englewood Cliffs, NJ: Prentice-Hall.

Mathis, W. & Trujillo, T. (eds.) (2016). *Learning from the Federal Market-Based Reforms*. Charlotte, NC: Information Age Publishing.

Mayhew, K. & Edwards, A. (1936). *The Dewey School*. New York: Appleton-Century.

McGill-Franzen, A. (2000). Policy and instruction: What is the relationship. In Kamil, M., Mosenthal, P., Pearson, P. D. & Barr, R. (eds). *Handbook on Reading Research*, vol. 3. Mahwah, NJ: Erlbaum.

Mearns, H. (1926). *Creative Youth*. New York: Doubleday.

Miller, G. A. (1965). Some preliminaries to psycholinguistics. *American Psychologist*, 20, 15–20.

Mills, H. (2014). *Learning for Real: Teaching Content and Literacy Across the Curriculum*. Portsmouth, NH: Heinemann.

Mills, H., O'Keefe, T., Hass, C. & Johnson, S. (2014). Changing hearts, minds, and actions through collaborative inquiry. *Language Arts*, 92, 36–51.

Mitchell, L. S. (1921). *Here and Now Story Book*. New York: Dutton.

Mitchell, L. S. (1924). *Here and Now Primer: Home from the Country*. New York: Dutton.

Mitchell, L. S. (1953). *Two Lives: The Story of Wesley Chair Mitchell and Myself*. New York: Simon & Schuster.

Mitra, D. & Serriere, S. (2015). *Civic Education in the Elementary Grades: Promoting Student Engagement in an Era of Accountability*. New York: Teachers College.

More, T. (1516). *Utopia*. Translated D. Price (1901), London, UK. Retrieved 11/16. http://www.gutenberg.org/files/2130/2130-h/2130-h.html

Morrell, E. (2014). Contexts, codes and cultures. *Language Arts*, 103, 12–15.

NAACP (National Association for the Advancement of Colored People) (2016). Criminal justice fact sheet. Retrieved 11/16. www.naacp.org/pages/criminal-justice-fact-sheet.

National Commission on Excellence in Education (NCEE) (1983). A nation at risk: The imperative for educational reform. NCEE, Washington, DC. Retrieved 11/16. www2.ed.gov/pubs/NatAtRisk/index.html

National Equity Project (2016). Reimagine leadership. Retrieved 01/17. http://nationalequityproject.org/home/reimagine-leadership

Naumburg, M. (1928a). *The Child and the World*. New York: Harcourt, Brace & Co.

Naumburg, M. (1928b). Progressive education. *The Nation*, 126, 343–344.

Naumburg, M. (1930). The crux of progressive education. *New Republic*, 63, 145–146.

Neef, J. (1808/1969). *Sketch of a Plan and Method of Education Founded on an Analysis of the Human Faculties and Natural Reason Suitable for the Offspring of a Free People and for all Natural Beings*. New York: Arno.

Nieves, E. (1997). Pupils' script on workers is ruled out. *New York Times*, June 26, Our Towns. Retrieved 11/16. www.nytimes.com/1997/06/26/nyregion/pupils-script-on-workers-is-ruled-out.html.

Norton, D., Henk, M., Fagin, B., Taylor, J. & Loeb, Z. (2012). Occupy Wall Street librarians speak out. *Progressive Librarian*, 38/39, 3–16.

Nyquist, E. (1972). Open education: Its philosophy, historical perspective, and implications. In E. Nyquist & G. Hawes (eds), *Open Education: A Sourcebook for Parents and Teachers*. New York: Bantam.

Oberholtzer, E. (1934). The Houston experiment. In G. Whipple (ed.), *The Activity Movement*. 33rd Yearbook of the National Society for the Study of Education. Part 2. Bloomington, IL: Public School Publishing.

Owocki, R. & Goodman, Y. (2002). *Kidwatching*. Portsmouth, NH: Heinemann.

Paller, R. (1997). Fifth graders do their own play on Broadway. *Playbill*, October 27. Retrieved 11/16. www.playbill.com/news/article/5th-graders-do-their-own-play-on-bway-oct.-27-71875

Parker, F. (1883). *Talks on Teaching*. New York: Kellogg.

Parker, F. (1884). *Talks on Pedagogics*. New York: Kellogg.

Parker, F. (1902). Editorial. *Elementary School Teacher*, 2, 754.

Patridge, L. (1885 [2010]). *The "Quincy Method" Illustrated: Penn Photographs from the Quincy Schools*. New York: Kellogg.

Pearson, P. D. (1989). Reading the whole language movement. *Elementary School Journal*, 90, 231–241.

Perl, S. & Wilson, N. (1986). *Through Teachers' Eyes: Portraits of Writing Teachers at Work*. Portsmouth, NH: Heinemann.

Pestalozzi, J. (1780). *Leonard and Gertrude*. Trans. by E. Channing. Boston: Heath (1897).

Pestalozzi, J. (1801). *How Gertrude Teaches her Children*. Trans. by L. Holland and F. Turner. Syracuse, NY: Bardeen (1909).

Pestalozzi, J. (1827). *Letters on Early Education*. Edited by R. Sherwood. London: Sherwood, Gilbert & Piper (1927).

Peterson, B. (2011). The birth of rethinking schools. *Rethinking Schools*, 26, 1, 1, 4.

Pratt, C. (1948). *I Learn from Children*. New York: Simon & Schuster.

Pratt, C. & Stanton, J. (1926). *Before Books*. Ann Arbor, MI: University of Michigan Press.

Ravitch, D. (2000). *Left Back: A Century of Failed School Reforms*. New York: Simon & Schuster.

Ravitch, D. (2010). *The Death and Life of the Great American School System: How Testing and Choice Are Undermining Education*. New York: Basic.

Reardon, S. (2011). The widening academic achievement gap between rich and poor. In G. Duncan & R. Murnane (eds), *Whither Opportunity? Rising Inequality, Schools, and Children's Life Chances*. New York: Russell Sage Foundation.

Redefer, F. (1948/49). Resolutions, reactions, and reminiscences. *Progressive Education*, 26, 178–197.

Rice, J. M. (1893). *The Public School System of the United States*. New York: Century. Retrieved 11/16. https://archive.org/details/publicschoolsys01ricegoog.

Rice, J. M. (1912). *The Scientific Management of Education*. New York: Hinds, Noble & Eldridge.

Rist, R. (1970). Student social class and teacher expectations. *Harvard Educational Review*, 40, 411–451.

Rivilin, A. & Timpane, M. (1967). *Should We Give Up or Try Harder? Planned Variation Education*. Washington, DC: Brookings Institute.

Rousseau, J. J. (1761). *Julie ou la nouvelle Héloïse*. Trans. by J. McDonell. University Park, PA: Pennsylvania State (1973).

Rousseau, J. J. (1762). *Emile*. Trans. by B. Foxley. London: Everyman (1972).

Rousseau, J. J. (1782). *Confessions*, vol. 1. London: Dent & Sons (1953).

Rowan, B. (2011). Intervening to improve the educational outcomes of students in poverty. In G. Duncan & R. Murnane (eds), *Whither Opportunity? Rising Inequality, Schools, and Children's Life Chances*. New York: Russell Sage Foundation.

Rugg, H. (1929). *An Introduction to American Civilization*. Boston: Ginn.

Rugg, H. (1931). *An Introduction to Problems in American Culture*. Boston: Ginn.

Rugg, H. (1932). *Changing Governments and Changing Cultures*. New York: Ginn.

Rugg, H. (1941). *So That Men May Understand*. New York: Doubleday, Doran & Co.

Rugg, H. & Counts, G. (1927). A critical appraisal of current methods of curriculum making. In G. Whipple (ed.), *The Foundation and Technique of Curriculum Construction*. 26th Yearbook of the National Society for the Study of Education, part 2. Bloomington, IL: Public School Publishing.

Rugg, H. & Shumaker, A. (1928). *The Child-Centered School: An Appraisal of a School Gardening the New Education*. Yonkers-on-Hudson, NY: World Book.

Sands, C., Reed, L., Harper, K. & Shar, M. (2009). A photovoice participatory evaluation of a school gardening program through the eyes of fifth graders. *Practicing Anthropology*, 31, 15–20.

Schwartz, A. & Stiefel, L. (2011). Immigrants and inequality in public schools. In G. Duncan & R. Murnane (eds), *Whither Opportunity? Rising Inequality, Schools, and Children's Life Chances*. New York: Russell Sage Foundation.

Serierre, S., Mitra, D. & Cody, J. (2010). Young citizens take action for better school lunches. *Social Studies and the Young Learner*, 23, 4–8.

Sewell, W. (2005). *Logics of History: Social History and Social Transformation*. Chicago: University of Chicago Press.

Shanahan, T. (2006). The national reading panel report: Practical advice for teachers. Learning Point Associates, Naperville, IL. Retrieved 11/16. www.learningpt.org/pdfs/literacy/nationalreading.pdf.

Shannon, P. (1989). *Broken Promises: Reading Instruction in 20th-Century America*. Granby, MA: Bergin & Garvey.

Shannon, P. (2007). *Reading against Democracy: Broken Promises in Reading Instruction*. Portsmouth, NH: Heinemann.

Shannon, P. (2011). *Reading Wide Awake: Politics, Pedagogies and Possibilities*. New York: Teachers College Press.

Shannon, P. (ed.) (2013). *Closer Readings of the Common Core*. Portsmouth, NH: Heinemann.

Shannon, P. (2014). *Reading Poverty in America*. New York: Routledge.

Shannon, P. (2015). It could be otherwise: Reading specialists and social justice. In J. Richards & K. Zenkov (eds), *Social Justice, the Common Core, and Closing the Instructional Gap*. Charlotte, NC: Information Age.

Simon, C. (2013). Disability studies: A new normal. *New York Times*, November 1, Education Life, 18–19.

Smarter Balanced Assessment Consortium (2014, November 14). Interpretation and use of scores and achievement levels: Regents of the University of California. Retrieved 11/16. www.smarterbalanced.org/wp-content/uploads/2015/08/Interpretation-and-Use-of-Scores.pdf

Smith, F. (1973). *Psycholinguistics and Reading*. New York: Holt, Rinehart & Winston.

Smith, N. B. (1934, 1967, 1987, 2002). *American Reading Instruction*. Newark, DE: International Reading Association.

Solomon, M. (2009). True adventures of students writing online: Mummies, vampires and schnauzers, oh my. In A. Herrington, K. Hodgson & C. Moran (eds), *Teaching the New Writing: Technology, Change and Assessment in the 21st-Century Classroom*. New York: Teachers College.

Staff of the Maury School (1941). *Teaching Reading in the Elementary School*. New York: The Progressive Education Association.

Stanton, E. C. (1882). The solitude of self. *The Women's Column*, January, 2–3. Retrieved 11/16. http://historymatters.gmu.edu/d/5315

Steward, C. (1922). *Moonlight Schools*. New York: Dutton.

Strauss, V. (2013). Arne Duncan: 'White suburban moms' upset that common core shows their kids aren't 'brilliant'. *Washington Post*, November 16. Retrieved 11/16. www.washingtonpost.com/news/answer-sheet/wp/2013/11/16/arne-duncan-white-surburban-moms-upset-that-common-core-shows-their-kids-arent-brilliant/

Strauss, V. (2015a). Report: Big education firms spend millions lobbying for pro-testing policies. *Washington Post*, March 30. Retrieved 11/16. www.washingtonpost.com/news/answer-sheet/wp/2015/03/30/report-big-education-firms-spend-millions-lobbying-for-pro-testing-policies/

Strauss, V. (2015b). Civil rights groups blast parents opting their kids out of high stakes tests: Why they are wrong. *Washington Post*, May 6. Retrieved 11/16. www.washingtonpost.com/news/answer-sheet/wp/2015/05/06/civil-rights-groups-blast-parents-opting-their-kids-out-of-high-stakes-tests-why-they-are-wrong/

Sweeney, M. (1997/1998). Justice, do it! *Rethinking Schools*, 12, 2, 3–4.

Talleyrand, C. (1791). *Report on Public Instruction*. Paris, France. Retrieved 11/16. www.gutenberg.org/ebooks/26336.

Taylor, K. (2014). New York State students post slight gains on tests. *New York Times*, August 14. Retrieved 11/16. www.nytimes.com/2014/08/15/nyregion/test-scores-in-new-york-state-inch-up-results-show.html.

Tenorio, R. (1986). Confessions of a kindergarten teacher: How I survived Scott Foresman. *Rethinking Schools*, 1, 1–2.

Tenorio, R. (1989). A vision in two languages: Reflections on a two-way bilingual program. *Rethinking Schools*, 4, 4, 11–12.

Tyler, R. (1936). Defining and measuring objectives of progressive education. *Educational Research Bulletin*, 15, 67–72.

Vigdor, J. L. (2011). School desegregation and the black-white test score gap. In G. Duncan & R. Murnane (eds), *Whither Opportunity? Rising Inequality, Schools, and Children's Life Chances*. New York: Russell Sage Foundation.

Ward, L. F. (1883). *Dynamic Sociology*. New York: Appleton & Co.

Washburne, M. (1883). *Col. Parker: The Man and the Educational Reformer*. New York: Kellogg.

Weber, R. M. (1970). A linguistic analysis of first-grade reading errors. *Reading Research Quarterly*, 5, 427–451.

Wells, I. B. (1895). The red record: Tabulated statitistics and alleged causes of lynching in the United States. Original pamphlet, Chicago. Retrieved 11/16. https://archive.org/stream/theredrecord14977gut/14977.txt

Whipple, G. (ed.) (1933). *The Activity Movement*. 33rd Yearbook of the National Society for the Study of Education, Part 2. Bloomington, IL: Public School Publishing.

White, H. (1978). *Tropics of Discourse: Essays in Cultural Criticism*. Baltimore, MD: Johns Hopkins University Press.

White, H. (2014). *The Practical Past: Flashpoints*. Evanston, IL: Northwestern University Press.

Williams, A. (2015). By any dreams necessary: Malcolm X and the problem of high stakes testing. *Huffington Post*, April 12. Retrieved 11/16. http://www.huffingtonpost.com/yohuru-williams/by-any-dreams-necessary-m_b_6648002.html

Wirtschafter, Z. (1968). Frantic letters and memos. In P. Lopate (ed.), *Journal of a Living Experiment*. Teachers & Writers Collaborative (1979).

Wiseman, J. (2015). Trans-Pacific partnership seen as door for foreign suits against US. *New York Times*, March 25, Business, B1.

Wollstonecraft, M. (1790). *A Vindication of the Rights of Men*. London: Johnson. Retrieved 11/16. http://lf-oll.s3.amazonaws.com/titles/991/Wollstonecraft_0532_EBk_v6.0.pdf

Wollstonecraft, M. (1792). *A Vindication of the Rights of Women*. Boston: Peter Edes. Retrieved 11/16. www.bartleby.com/144/

Wood, G. (2010). In defense of academic history writing. *Perspectives on History*. April. Retrieved 11/16. www.historians.org/publications-and-directories/perpsectives-on-history/april2010/in-defense-of-academic-history-writing

INDEX

Whole Language Umbrella 92–93
Williams, A. 119
Williams, V. 86
Williamsburg, MA schools 110
Wirschafter, Z. 90
Wiseman, J. 115

Wollstonecraft, M. 24–26, 118, 121
Wood, G. 12
World is Flat, The (Friedman) 97
Writer's Laboratory 67

Zechiel, H. 71